. . . when we talk about **Raymond Carver**

. . . WHEN WE TALK ABOUT
RAYMOND CARVER

Conversations with

Maryann Carver
Richard Ford
Chuck Kinder
William Kittredge
Jay McInerney
Leonard Michaels
Robert Stone
Douglas Unger
Geoffrey Wolff
Tobias Wolff

Edited by Sam Halpert

First Edition

95 94 93 92 91 5 4 3 2 1

This is a Peregrine Smith Book, published by Gibbs Smith, Publisher P.O. Box 667, Layton, Utah 84041

Jacket design by R.D. Scudellari

Book design by Randall Smith Associates

Typography by Design Type Service

Manufactured in the United States of America

Library of Congress Cataloging-in-Publication Data

. . . when we talk about Raymond Carver / Interviews conducted by Sam Halpert.
    p. cm.
    ISBN 0-87905-377-1 : $17.95 FPT
    1. Carver, Raymond—Friends and associates—Interviews.
2. Carver, Raymond—Criticism and interpretation. 3. Authors, American—20th century—Biography. I. Halpert, Sam
PS3553.A7894Z97 1991
813'.54—dc20   9022139
                                               CIP

For T. and Michael, Susan, Rob;
and Daniel, Adam, Joel, Julianna

CONTENTS

INTRODUCTION

It was a long drive home in the Nissan pickup from the 1989 writer's conference in Squaw Valley, California, to my home in South Miami. Those abstract rectangular shapes on the roadmap became the abiding reality of endless stretches of Nevada, Utah, and New Mexico mountain and desert; and there is perhaps no better way to grasp the concept of infinity, than to drive across Oklahoma in August. The dark red setting sun spanned half the horizon behind me, as I slogged my way along the Interstate. I sang all the Hank Williams songs I knew two or three times over; then devised character, plot, and theme for what could have become, with just a little fine tuning, some of the greatest short stories of our time.

I ran three or four Raymond Carver stories through my mind. Carver had died the previous summer, and so many of the writers at Squaw Valley had expressed their high regard for him. It could begin with a sad reference to Carver's untimely death, or a reminiscence of an experience shared—a day, a week, a year, a time. Many wild tales were told of the "Bad Raymond" days, but all agreed that Ray never felt happier, or more fortunate, than when sharing time with friends and fellow writers.

He was a sensitive, compassionate man. You knew that from his stories. It can't be faked. His art was in the apparent simplicity of his work; in story after story. The opening sentence of "Where Is Everyone?" is compelling in its simplicity—"I've seen some things." A brief sentence, and we know Carver's people. The narrator in "What We Talk About When We Talk About Love" says, "We lived in Albuquerque then. But we were all from somewhere else."

I'd been hooked on writers' conferences ever since attending my first, three years earlier in Port Townsend, Washington. I drove cross-country from my home in South Miami specifically to meet Carver, who was to participate in the conference. When he heard that, he shook his head as if unable to absorb such data, then mumbled, "From Miami, Jesus!" I told him that I had read all his work since '76 when I first picked up *Will You Please Be Quiet, Please?*, and just couldn't put it down. Ray grinned, then gripped my arm and said in that low rumble of his, "Hey, one hell of a title."

He listened patiently as I told him how I'd thrust that book on all those not quick enough to cross the street at my approach. That had been a crazy time for me, right after my wife's decision to abandon her twenty-year experiment with my version of marriage. A guy, who I now realize was a true friend, told me it was the kick in the ass I had coming to me for years, and he hoped I'd learned a lesson from it. I felt betrayed. I had given him my last copy of *What We Talk About When We Talk About Love*. He never returned the book. Ray listened as if that was the greatest story ever, then told me to write it before he did. He chuckled, clapped me on the back, and drifted off to the smorgasbord.

At Port Townsend the following summer, I met Leonard Michaels. It was a good place. We became friends and had some fine times. We drank, shot pool, and swapped stories of earlier lives, often veering dangerously close to the truth, if it wouldn't hurt our story too much. Michaels saw me on the chow line one day, and suggested that I accompany him for a proper lunch in town. On the way in, he told me that Ray Carver might join us, was it okay? I assured him it was okay, I didn't mind. When they met, Ray embraced Lenny as if he'd just been paroled. I didn't stay long afterward, as I could see they had their own agenda, but I still recall Ray's mumbled greeting to me, "Hey, Miami, how's the work going?"

He was accompanied by his slightly seasick French editor. Ray said that they'd been fishing on his boat, when the editor, who had never fished before, had somehow snagged a forty pound salmon. It took two guys to clamp a hold on him to keep him from being pulled overboard. Richard Ford told me he was one of those guys when I interviewed him for this book.

It was only a few months later, in October, that Ray was told he had lung cancer. He died the following summer on August 2, 1988.

The long trip in the pickup from Squaw Valley took place the following year. I stopped for lunch in a cafe at Dumas, Arkansas, where a tired, older version of a Marlboro man was trying to rein in his temper in a dispute he was having with the woman who ran the place. I heard him tell her that there was no point in discussing that ol' Cadillac. She might just as well save her breath. He was the one who kept up the payments, he had the registration, and he had the keys, no matter what the fuck kind of court paper she had. She told him that we'll see what the sheriff has to say about that. He shifted gears and wondered if a man could sleep over in his own house just one night, where they'd have a chance to settle matters in a proper, dignified way. Courtney, grow up, she said, and busied herself at the coffee maker.

Hours later, driving through a rainy night in Mississippi, and damn near hypnotized by the slapping wiper blades, I speculated on how Carver might have treated that scene back there in Dumas. The rain tapered off, and I pulled to the side of the empty highway for a breather. I got out, stretched my legs, leaned against the Nissan, stared at the clouds sliding swiftly past a half moon, then came up with the idea of interviewing writers to discover what they talk about when they talk about Raymond Carver. It came, not in a blazing flash, but with the palpable sense that it had been there all along.

So there's the conception of this book. The tape recorded interviews were extemporaneous and unrehearsed. Transcriptions were sent to each writer for editing, and were invariably returned with little delay, many with old snapshots and messages of enthusiasm for the project. All generously contributed time and effort in spirited appreciation of Carver's work; their affection for him as a man permeated each interview. The entire process has been most heartening and, no other way of saying it, a labor of love. It was indeed regrettable that just as we were going to press, Tess Gallagher withdrew her interview from the book.

Special thanks to friend and soul mate Bob Scudellari who designed the jacket; to Bill Heyen for introducing me to Tess Gallagher to begin with; to my key grips, Jean Pugh, Peter Parsons, Tim Schmand; and of course to all those I interviewed, the good people who wrote this book for me.

Sam Halpert
South Miami, Florida

THE INTERVIEWS

Ray Carver, Robert Stone,
Jordan Bond, Tobias Wolff,
and Morris Bond with fish.

TOBIAS WOLFF

... people have taken this as a reference to Ray's own imminent death, but, in fact, he wrote this essay ["Friendship"] before he knew he had cancer, just as he wrote the story "Errand" about the death of Chekhov, before he knew he had cancer. We are all dying. We should all know that, but Ray knew it better than most.

We meet in Wolff's hotel room in Miami. He is here to give a reading at the annual Book Fair. He suggests that we discuss the ground rules for the interview. I suggest breakfast in the hotel coffee shop. The rules are established in a few minutes during our Florida Sunrise Breakfast Special. When we return to his room I tell him how much I admired his tribute to Ray in *Esquire*, September, 1989. We discuss Ray's moving little memoir, "Friendship" [*Granta 25*, Autumn, 1988]. He passes on a couple of anecdotes about Ray and then tells me how much he enjoys Miami— "no other city like it in the world." He draws the blinds open for a spectacular view of the bay and ocean. It is a beautiful day.

Sam Halpert: In his essay "Friendship," published shortly after his death, Carver writes on how he first met you and Richard Ford, and how much he treasured the friendship that grew from that meeting. There is a picture of the three of you, and Carver writes, "Boy, are these guys having fun!" Later in the essay, ". . . Things wind down. Things do come to an end. People stop living. Chances are that two of the three friends in this picture will have to gaze upon the remains—the remains—of the third friend, when that time comes. The thought is grievous, and terrifying. But the only alternative to burying your friends is that they will have to bury you." Could you give us your sense of this piece?

Tobias Wolff: I think it is a very interesting essay, full of a sense of mortality, a meditation about death, about how death will eventually end this friendship. And people have taken this as a reference to Ray's own imminent death, but in fact he wrote this essay before he knew he had cancer, just as he wrote the story "Errand," about the death of Chekhov, before he knew he had cancer. We are all dying. We should all know that, but Ray knew it better than most.

My recollections are mostly the same as his, except that I actually did meet him before the time he mentions in the essay. I think it was dramatically convenient for Ray to use our meeting up in Vermont. He was drinking when we first met, and so I don't think he remembered it very well. We were out in Palo Alto at the same time back in 1976.

What were you doing there then?

I was teaching at Stanford, and he had been living in the area for a few years then. He was already among the best of the young writers around, even though he wasn't much known by the public at that time. He was still having a hard time placing his stories in literary magazines, because they were considered rather odd and old-fashioned—which they aren't but were read that way because they weren't in the experimental mode of fiction that inhabits the pages of literary journals of ten years ago or so. I was very familiar with his work, and most of my friends were. We'd meet at parties, but he was a drunk at the time. He'd be funny, vibrant, but he wasn't very sensible to his surroundings. He was a different person later on. We really didn't get to know each other until the time he recounts in his essay and I recount in mine [*Esquire,* September 1989]. We only have certain moments in our lives when we can get to know a person well. These moments get fewer and fewer as we get older because of the demands of work and family. Ray and I had that opportunity in Vermont. This was like summer camp—winter camp. We were up there in Vermont in this dormitory for two weeks together. Both of us were night owls and we'd sit up and drink coffee and just talk all night like kids and it was wonderful. We got to know each other well. We did this for a couple of years—in each other's company for long periods of uninterrupted time.

Who were some of the other writers teaching there then?

Well, it was really an extraordinary place. Richard Ford was there,

John Irving, Craig Nova, Stephen Dobyns, Michael Ryan, Ellen Voigt, Donald Hall, Louise Gluck, Robert Hass, many others.

What year was this?

These were the years '78 to '80.

Then this was when your friendship started rather than when you first met Ray in Palo Alto?

Yes.

Ray's last published story, "Errand," that you mentioned earlier, has a far different style than any of his previous stories. Do you believe this represents a change of direction in his work?

Well, as you'll notice in the story, he comes back to what is very characteristic of his writing—the experience of an ordinary person, the waiter, in an extraordinary circumstance. He doesn't know what is happening and his life is illuminated by something he cannot fathom. He's carrying the burden of history for a moment. It seems to me that Ray's interest in the end was almost more with this guy than it was with Chekhov. Whether or not this story represents a change of direction in his work, I can't say. I rather think not, because of the other stories he was writing at the time, like "Blackbird Pie" and "Who's Been Sleeping In This Bed?" and "Elephant." I don't think his work would have changed so much in that he would have written about historical figures, but there is a change in the spirit of his stories. His earlier work is hard-edged and exact, and there isn't very much of what I'd call the spirit of kindness in the voice, though I love those stories still. I still read his stories of that period. They remind me of *Dubliners.* They have that same detachment, but later on there's a moderation in the tone, a gentleness, a spiritual restlessness, and a profound compassion for the people he's writing about. That's the way I see his work—I don't want to use the term *developing* because it seems to suggest that one thing is preferable over the other. It isn't—it's just different; but his work was changing.

I always found it interesting to read the latest Carver story, because it was always going to be a little different than the last one. I remember reading "Cathedral" for the first time. I was lying on a couch, and I had the feeling when I came to the end of that story that I was levitating. Literally, of course, I wasn't, but I felt like I was levitating. I was so charged by the story and drawn up by it that I ran to the phone and spent about half an hour trying to track Ray down. I finally found him at Yaddo, and I had to tell him at that moment what he'd done. I just wanted him to hear from another writer what a masterpiece he had written. I can't think of too many times when I've read work that made me want to do that.

After you began your friendship with him in Vermont, how did you keep in touch?

We were never really much out of touch after that. At that time, when we weren't in Vermont we were both in Arizona. He and Tess Gallagher were living in Tucson, and I was living with my wife, Catherine, in Phoenix. We used to exchange visits. When Ray started teaching in Syracuse, he suggested they hire me and Tess as well because they were putting their writing program back together again. It had been a very distinguished writing program, but a number of people had retired and died. From 1980 on we were all at Syracuse together. The Strauss Living Award in 1984 allowed him to stop teaching, but he kept the house in Syracuse because Tess was still teaching there. We were in constant touch throughout the year. And he loved to talk on the phone. He was very boyish in that way. I notice this in my sons, this almost physical appetite for contact with their friends. You have that when you're young. It usually wanes when you get older, but Ray never lost it.

That's the way it comes across in "Friendship"—that you and he and Richard Ford are just good old buddies.

Well, that's the way he was. He *was* a buddy, and he liked having his buddies around him.

You must have struck a chord in him, because he couldn't possibly be like that with everybody.

No, he wasn't like that with everybody, but it was amazing to watch how quickly he made friends. He was a very sweet man, a very plain man, and he had a friendly feeling toward people. Let me give you an example. There's a poem of his called "Luck" about two boys at a house where a party is going on, and they get excited by the noise and the drinking. They go out and spend the night in the woods and come back the next morning and everyone's gone, the house is a shambles, and drinks are all around the house. The narrator, the poet, pours all the drinks together and says, "Friends, I thought this was living. A house where no one was home, and all I could drink." Notice the word "friends," the way he uses that word. With most writers, it would be an affectation, but it wasn't with him. That was his address to the world.

Could you tell us about your last visit with Ray?

Yes, he came over to the house for a Christmas celebration. He was then recovering from his operation for lung cancer. A couple of nights earlier, he'd been to a party at Stephen Dobyns's house, and he'd been dancing. Everybody thought, "Great, Ray's back in the saddle again." So we were in a mood to celebrate. About a week after that I left for Germany for a year, and Ray went out west to Washington with Tess. Then the cancer came back. I guess that's the way it works. Ray probably could have informed himself better of how all this was going to go. From what I now understand, the type of lung cancer he had almost always comes back. There are very few cases where it does not. But even while he was about to go into surgery, he took care not to inform himself about this. He practiced what they call denial, and I was and am all in favor of that. It kept his spirits up to think that he was going to be cured. He never let people talk about it when they'd come over to the house. We'd sit around and joke and laugh. He'd laugh and gossip and ignore his sickness. He just wasn't interested in it. I think that was all to the good, because he was able to keep writing. He was able to stay happy and hopeful. When the cancer came back, he kept it to himself as much as possible. He wanted to keep working, and he didn't want a flock of mourners descending upon him. Everybody had gathered around him when he got sick in the fall. There was no reason to repeat that. The important thing for him was to get his work done, so he kept it to himself and kept on working. A very brave man.

Was this the period when he wrote the poem "What The Doctor Said," which begins with "He said it doesn't look good / he said it looks bad in fact real bad" and ends with "I may even have thanked him habit being so strong"?

Oh, yes. He had a very macabre sense of humor and that comes out in that poem, too.

Is there any single piece of his that you prefer over the others? A favorite story or poem perhaps?

I can't really do that. I loved so much of his work. That's the thing about Ray—he was never not himself. I can't think of a story of his that doesn't bring him sharply into my mind. I have many favorites, but among the favorites I cannot make any distinction. I love "Cathedral." I love "A Small, Good Thing."

Which version of "A Small, Good Thing?"

Not the short version, the one called "The Bath." That was actually the only story he wrote that I didn't like. When it came out in his collection *What We Talk About When We Talk About Love*, I didn't care for it at all, but I loved what he did to it later in "A Small, Good Thing." There's "Feathers," and the stories in his first collection that I still treasure like "We're Not Your Husband" and "The Idea" and "Put Yourself In My Shoes," many others.

And "So Much Water So Close To Home"?

When I start naming my favorite Carver story, what's going to happen is I will name them all.

Do you find his poems very much like his stories?

The voice is the same, but the poems are more personal than the stories.

If you won't single out a story or poem of Ray's as your favorite, could you perhaps recall a scene or section that stands out in your mind as characteristically Carver's?

He has a poem called "The Baker," that I've always thought of as something very—how can I put it—I felt that Ray's heart was right there in that poem, and his wisdom, and his experience of life. It's about a baker in Mexico who lives in a little town where Ray invents a meeting between Count Vronsky, Anna Karenina's lover who is acting as a mercenary in the Mexican Revolution, and Pancho Villa. They meet at the baker's house. They both become interested in his wife, and she's sitting in Pancho Villa's lap and kissing him on the ear. They're talking about women and horses and getting drunker and drunker with their pistols out. The poor baker is terrified, and in the morning when he gets up and they're asleep, he takes his shoes and sneaks out of the house. At the end Ray says that this baker—humiliated, terrified, running for his life—he is the hero of this poem. That goes to the heart of Ray's sense of life, that rejection of the heroic and lofty. The virtue of endurance, just staying alive in this world, Ray honors that in his work. Poetry gives Ray the chance to speak directly. He speaks in another way in his stories—metaphorically, you might say. The stories are equivalents of some condition he wants to write about.

In the story "Are These Actual Miles?" when Leo sends his wife out to sell the car and he's walking around the house and he's even thinking about hanging himself, Ray writes that "Leo understood that he was willing to be dead." That's such a devastating line to read. There's no way of articulating that condition without having felt it. Then in "Cathedral," the scene when he has that blind man's hand and he's guiding it through the motions . . . Scene after scene comes back to me.

Though I know Ray's work very well, in the end it's very difficult for me to isolate moments. He is not a particularly quotable writer. That's one of his virtues, that he never tried to achieve a beautiful line. It's the steadiness and quietness of his prose that creates his sense of reality. You never get the feeling, "Oh, yeah, the writer got off a good one there." That's never in his work. I can read things that are more brilliant on the surface, but they don't go to the heart of things the way Ray's work does. He gets there in a very quiet, unassuming way, but he's only apparently simple. It takes art to do what he does.

So much of what he writes seems drawn from his experience. In "Vitamins," for instance . . .

Why do you say you know that really happened to him?

Are you turning this around?

No, I get to ask questions, too. Why did you say that?

I'd say because it's written so well, so true. Not journalistic, but the details are there, and the feeling, and the humiliation of the man. You can't just imagine these.

Well, suppose I tell you that this didn't happen to Ray.

Then I would have to say that if it didn't happen to him, then it had to happen to someone he knew very well.

Are you talking about the literal circumstances of the story? You see, I think you have to make a distinction between his work and his life. Ray was an artist. He was a creator, not a self-biographer. He used elements of his life in his work, but he didn't simply transcribe them. This is not an autobiographical story. What is autobiographical in this story is the spiritual condition that he describes of humiliation and fear and moral drift. That's what's real in the story; otherwise it's a fiction. A good writer should make you feel as if he lived the story he is telling. But at the end of the story, we always have to draw back and say, "This was a story." If it were a memoir, Ray would have called it a memoir. When people immediately assume his work was autobiographical, it takes something away from his artistic achievement. It is an artistic achievement to make someone feel they have had an encounter with reality, when what they have had an encounter with is a writer's imagination. I mean, look at Ray's story "Night School" in his first collection. There again we have the feeling of somebody telling something he actually did, but that's not in fact the case. That is a made-up story. So you have to be very careful about attributing to Ray experiences he wrote about, simply because he wrote about them so well. This is an important point, because people often talk this way about Ray's work, as if it were all simply his life story. He certainly would use anything—he'd use things from my life, he'd use things from Tess's life, from his friends' lives without any scruple at all, as well as from his own, but he wasn't writing his own biography.

As in the story "Elephant," where the narrator tells of his family members sponging on him?

There may be things in there that are autobiographical, but they aren't in the end the story.

And in "Intimacy," where the narrator goes back to talk with his ex-wife. Could that actually have happened?

It may have happened in his mind. I'll bet a lot of these things happened in Ray's mind, but that's as real as anything else. The big thing is that the stories are authentic. They are real stories; and whether or not they happened exactly in that way to him—well, who cares? If we want to know what happened to him, we can always find out, because he was never shy about telling us. He wrote about his life in the essay "Fires." He wrote about it in his memoir of his father. He wrote about it in his poetry.

Then he would use his experience for his art without coloring it?

Of course he colored it. He was an artist. He colored everything.

What do you mean by coloring?

When you simply transcribe reality, it isn't real anymore. You get the Watergate tapes. You get something without any continuity or substance. That's why when people try to write they find it so difficult. They think, "I'll just put this down the way it happened." But there's something missing. And it is exactly that coloration that Ray brings to his writing. He has a take on the world. The things that happened to him are not just set down. They're organized according to the way he sees life; his vision of life colors everything he wrote. So it isn't passed on as a neutral transcription of experience. It is individualistic, personal, subjective. That's what I mean by colored; but please note that it's your word, not mine.

I suppose if there is some heat in my response, it is because I am sensitive to hearing Ray spoken of simply as a man who wrote about his own hard life. That is not why his fiction is so powerful. I've read many stories of hard lives and they generally leave me cold. I am unmoved because they have not been turned into art. The private becomes public in the realm of art, and unless it can be turned into art it remains private. That's what Ray was able to accomplish. He was a great artist, a great artist.

Then those critical of his work misunderstand this?

I think so. I believe they don't make a distinction between the life and the work. They don't make a distinction between the man and the artist. He was an artist. Like most writers, Ray was not above cultivating a certain myth about himself, and that may contribute somewhat to the way people read his life into his stories. The fact of the matter is they are different things. I would like to see Ray regarded as the great artist he was, and not as somebody who had a terrible life that he wrote about.

Hasn't he become the focus of the attack on minimalism or the so-called K-Mart fiction?

That's true. He has been a lightning rod drawing that criticism. Well, we should all be so lucky as to be considered the head of the column to be attacked. First of all I don't think he ever used the word K-Mart in any of his fiction. *[Pause.]* You know, I'm not going to dignify this by discussing it. I just find this whole minimalism thing—or as it's called in England, "dirty realism"—a perversely uninteresting way of reading. It's a way of talking about writers without reading them carefully is what it really is. The minute you start talking about other people as though they were one, you know you're in trouble, and that goes for writers as well. I don't like categories. They talk about the moderns. They talk about Joyce, they talk about Fitzgerald and Faulkner and Hemingway using that term. What the hell do they have to do with each other? I mean, really, they're all completely different, and the only thing they have in common is they lived in about the same time. They teach courses on the moderns in the universities, so no doubt some day they'll teach courses on the minimalists, and that will be just as stupid.

What do you believe Ray's position will be in literature?

Well, first of all anything I say on this is obviously complete speculation because we don't ever know what will happen. But I have a strong suspicion that Ray will be one of those writers who will be read with care and love as long as people read our language. He has penetrated a secret about us and brought it to the light, and he does it again and again. You have to go to the water and drink. There's something pure and cool and honest in his vision of life, and the beauty of his language, its exactness, its cadences, and its music. People will go back to it again and again and again.

November 22, 1989
Miami, Florida

*Ray Carver in Syracuse,
N.Y. in 1986 or 1987.*

LEONARD MICHAELS

*Michaels: Well, what can I say? When Ray was low,
he got drunk. When I was low, I read Hegel.*

Halpert: Hegel! You had no other choice?

*Michaels: Well, neither of us were too happy at the
time.*

The interview begins in Michaels's office at the University of California in Berkeley. It is a small utilitarian room; unpretentious, books on shelves floor to ceiling, overflowing on to three chairs and a desk with portable typewriter in the center of the room. After a short break for lunch, we continue the interview at his small, comfortable house in Kensington, a few minutes' drive from campus. We are greeted by his eleven-year-old daughter, who gives her dad an affectionate hug and kiss. Lenny beams as he embraces his favorite critic.

Sam Halpert: When and where did you first meet Ray?

Leonard Michaels: I don't remember exactly when, but he was in my living room, here in Kensington, sometime in the early seventies. He got in touch with me. He got in touch because we had friends in common and he said he'd like to visit. I think that's how it went. I said sure and he came by. Here was this very nicely dressed, very composed—and, it seemed to me, tensely restrained—soft-spoken man, a little on the burly side perhaps. I remember him sitting in the living room, staring at me, waiting for something to be said, or something to happen. He had this quality of patient waiting, not putting himself forward, letting you determine the direction of talk. He wore a gray tweed jacket, I believe. He also wore a tie and neatly pressed pants. I might have taken him for a businessman, maybe an insurance salesman. His composure, his conventional clothes—as if he'd come for a job interview. I can't remember one word of our conversation, but he made a very good impression. A solid kind of guy. Salt of the earth. I never met anyone who seemed more *normal*.

Had you read any of his stories prior to meeting him?

I can't recall, but I must have read a story or two and thought they were good. Around then I was editing a magazine called *Occident*, or acting as one of the editors. It was the University of California literary, the oldest literary journal in the state. I asked Ray to give us a story.

Did you publish it?

Yes. It was his early work, and I liked it a lot. I liked his sense of humor and the way he managed to suppress a certain element of rationality, so the events in a story would move forward by virtue of a subconscious compulsion. As if there were no reality principle. This is too complicated and I don't like to talk this way. There was a craziness in his stories that pleased me. I never made the connection between his stories—how they move from the normal to the weirdly extravagant—and his personality. On some level I felt the dynamic in them and him, and I liked it.

And after that . . .

After that Ray needed a job. I used what influence I had to get him something here at Berkeley. Then I tried to make Berkeley extend itself and keep him on, give him some kind of security, but that didn't work out. He wasn't a star, he wasn't fashionable, he didn't have a Ph.D., he was just another writer coming up. Besides there was opposition from one of my fellow writers in the department. He said his work was remorselessly downbeat. It should have been more cheery and optimistic, maybe like Beckett and Kafka. The more people attacked Ray, the more I realized he was an important writer.

After that I tried to help Ray get a Guggenheim fellowship. I typed out a long letter, essentially saying that I was aware the foundation didn't usually grant fellowships the first time somebody applied for one, but let me try to tell you what I believe is important about his writing. My point was that this is rare and this should be supported. I thought I'd written the most irresistible plea ever.

[Laughter. Pause.] If you look at Ray's first book you'll see an endorsement from just one writer.

Well, we know you're the world's greatest critic. [Laughter.] *Did Ray do well after the book came out?*

Yes, but there were heavy blows at first. A number of established sensibilities didn't want him in the city. There's a Russian saying: "When you enter the city, the geese begin to cackle." But then some big names weighed in on his side. Soon thereafter right opinion seized the mental masses, high and low.

What did you think of his work after that?

There are impressive stories early and late, but I like the early stuff—a lot of it anyway—best. It had a wild, musical quality. Like poetry, but you know you don't find much of this wildness in Ray's poetry.

Do you find that note missing in his later work?

No, it's not missing. It's just that his work becomes deeper, almost as if he begins to feel what he feels, so the meaning of the stories is *in* the stories, whereas in the first book the meaning can wait. Do you see what I mean? The story has trajectory. The meaning can come along later. It's not so involved in the experience of the story itself. Take a late story like *Intimacy,* where Ray is being naughty, isn't he? I mean the naughty character who resembles Ray in the story, and Ray himself, outside the story. The feeling of all that is part of the story's self-consciousness. Maybe if I didn't know the people, I wouldn't find it problematic, or maybe the story is disturbing to me just because it is a good story. His later work is, for all I know, superior. I'm talking about what I like. I'm not talking about what's good or bad in the eye of God.

Are you saying his early work is more visceral? Purer?

It's more musical. To my ear. More terrifying. Terrifying in the Kierkegaardian sense, like life itself. I don't know. *[Laughs.]* Forget that.

15

You also knew him on a more personal level.

We were friends. I didn't see him regularly over a long period, but he invited me to parties at his house, and I invited him to parties in Berkeley, and there were other occasions when we talked, just talked without any formal context.

What was your sense of him, let's say, when you met him at a party?

My sense of him was that he was often drunk—not in a flamboyant way, just a little sodden. I never saw him become angry or violent. He always remained pleasant, even funny, except one time in Santa Cruz. I remember him slumped in a big chair in the living room of his house while the party was going full blast, and he was gloomily studying the crowd, the people dancing. He dealt with alcoholism in his stories. I assume it's his own experience. I don't mean he's writing exactly what it is that happens to him in the course of his own life. He may well have done that, for all I know, but he obviously was using his knowledge of certain kinds of experience at a very deep level. The stories do have that sort of confessional force. This is—what can I say—*[pause]* an argument for some people.

An argument for what?

You know, people whisper that the story is the truth, or it's based on reality and so on and so forth, and you're supposed to believe that the story is less of an achievement somehow, that it's less of a creative thing. Well, the quality of a story is in *how* it is written, not what the story is about; anyhow, stories just don't come out of nowhere, like the world came out of nowhere. Before God came along, there was nothing. God didn't have any experience, right?

Maybe that's what's wrong with the world.

[Laughs.] Wait until the next time around. It's going to be terrific!

In the revision?

Yes, it's all in the rewrite.

What else was going on in his life at the time?

Well, I heard that he was teaching at Iowa and Santa Cruz without informing either school about his job at the other. He even managed to con United into flying him for free, telling them he'd put United into his stories. Of course he never wrote a word about them. He also had a lover in Denver where he changed planes. So there he was, holding on to two teaching jobs a couple of thousand miles apart, and drinking, and carrying on a love affair, and conning United into flying him back and forth. Anyway that's what I heard. There's much more gossip, but it has no real relation to his writing. It's just life. Material. Stuff. Of interest to media-besotted types who can't read.

How were you getting along with him at that time?

Well, there was a party—it was right after the publication of my second book. Ray drew me aside and told me straight out exactly what he didn't like in the book. He didn't like the literary allusions, references to philosophers, or explicit statement of ideas. I'd heard this before from other writers. These things in my writing took away from the brainless pitch of reality. There was no drama or pleasure in them. Why did I do it? Ray disapproved. I had done it for a reason other than he imagined. It was intended to represent states of depression, not intellectuality. He hurt my feelings, especially since he'd once said I was an influence on his own writing, but my point in telling this is to show how he was changing, gaining confidence. Anyway, this is not about me.

But it is, you and Ray.

Well, what can I say? When he was low, he got drunk. When I was low, I read Hegel.

Hegel! [Laughs.] *You had no other choice?*

Well, neither of us were too happy at the time.

Did he have more than a drinking problem at that time?

I spent afternoons and evenings with him and Maryann, and I could see the kind of trouble they were having, but I also saw that they were deeply connected in ways that are almost impossible to describe. They were very close. I can't get into this. I can't say what goes on in anybody's marriage in the real world; I make things up when I write.

17

But there were things that I could see about that marriage that suggested to me, however bad it may have been, the very badness came out of some tremendously deep, intimate, absolute condition, something very important to both of them—but they were both involved in it. I loved them both and I saw they had trouble, and I saw they were deeply—and it looked to me, permanently—connected.

Was Maryann with him at these parties during the Bad Raymond days?

Yes. He was always with Maryann. There was one time he arrived with Maryann, Bill Kittredge, Doug Unger, and I don't know who else. This was at the party celebrating Ray's story in *Occident*. I remember they came walking in, Maryann first, and she was clearly bombed out of her mind. I thought she had arrived alone, but ten seconds later Kittredge came walking in, also bombed, and both of them smiling in a pleasing drunken way, and I thought, well, at least Kittredge and Maryann arrived. Next thing I know, along comes Unger. Now all these people had come together to the party, but they were walking in at ten-second intervals, and not as a joke. This was just how they were arriving in their separate little worlds, and finally along comes Ray, smiling just the way he always smiled. There they were, *[laughs]* one after the other in single file, shuffling across the room to say hello. I almost always saw him with Maryann.

With all that drunkenness, how did he create those stories?

He found the material for his stories in the things that were happening to him, the things he was seeing and feeling. The people he dealt with and lived with were all participants in a way in his writing. I imagine Maryann lived through a hell of a lot of that material with him, and I suspect that she *and* Ray paid for those stories with their lives.

Could you tell us a bit more about Maryann?

She was always quick to say what she thought when she didn't like something. A writer's name would come up and she might say, "There's nobody home," meaning the work was shit. Ray never disagreed, but he wouldn't put himself on record—at least, not around me. He was cautious, diplomatic. Saying what you think, even in the most innocent circumstances, can come back to haunt you later. Maryann wasn't diplomatic. She was strong, forthright, even a little fierce. As far as I could tell, she was right in her judgments. Ray was lucky to have her reading his work, just to keep it free of schmaltz and manipulation.

Could you say something about the misunderstanding you once had with Ray?

I wrote a letter asking him to write an essay for a book I was doing. In the letter I reminded him of one of the parties and made a big joke out of it. I have a feeling that letter irritated him. He didn't want to be reminded. He didn't want to be reminded in the way that I reminded him. I think that was it. I'm not sure. I was very lighthearted and laughing when I wrote the letter, and I thought he'd get a big kick out of it, but he never made any reference to it. So I decided it was a stupid letter, the wrong thing to do. I didn't fully understand what was going on in his life. Naturally we never mentioned that letter. I still have it and look at it every now and then and regret it.

Did you ever get the essay?

No. He was completely and legally bound to the *New Yorker* at that point. He couldn't do anything without offering it to them first. He seemed to be very happy to have this contract. It represented some kind of . . . *[Pause, searching for a word.]*

Security?

I don't think it was security but more like acknowledgment that he had arrived. Like getting a diploma, maybe. He marveled at the amount of money they gave him for signing the contract: seven thousand dollars. He said the number as if it were a thing, a miracle number-thing that had dropped into his life. I suppose, after all he had been through, any good thing still surprised him, so he spoke in a tone that suggested he couldn't understand how this was happening to an ordinary, unlucky guy like himself. He wasn't all that awed. He may have intended to sound that way only to hold off the demonic forces, the ones that are sure to punish you if you take any pleasure in anything in your life.

I remember seeing Ray greet you so warmly, embracing you, in Port Townsend one day in August '87. What was that all about?

I hadn't seen Ray for a very long time. There had been that one bit of communication—that letter—which was a mistake as I've said. He came by to visit me in Port Townsend from his house in Port Angeles, and I was very glad that he had, because in a way, to tell you the truth, I felt forgiven for having written that stupid letter. I was very glad to see him, glad when he stepped out of his—was it a Mercedes? You were there.

Yes, a brown Mercedes.

When we first met, he owned a VW bug. It was always strewn with unpaid traffic tickets and emergency room receipts and other such evidence of the high-stress little miseries of his daily life. His Mercedes was clean. His big hug told me we were friends—there was no ill feeling. But there was one other reason that I suspected there might be some negative element in our friendship. It had to do with the fact that I was once asked to judge a writing contest. I had this huge pile of manuscripts, and I was going crazy trying to do the job, trying to read through this pile of stuff. And Ray called up in the middle of it and said, "I hear you're judging this so-and-so writing contest," and I said yes. And he said, "Well, you know so-and-so has submitted a manuscript." And I said, "Yes, it's true, I've seen his name." And Ray said, "Well, he's really a very good writer" and blah, blah. Anyhow, that made it impossible for me to give this guy the prize. I don't know that I would have, but I do know I might have. And after Ray's phone call I was so totally fucked up, that all I could think of was, "Now if I give this guy the prize, I'll never know if I'd acted in an honest way." So I ended up not doing it and feeling compromised. That was a negative thing. Years went by and, what can I say—aaagh—it was awful. And then the next thing was this letter. Maybe my stupid letter was a bit hostile. It may have been a hostile letter, though I thought it was hilariously funny. He didn't think so one bit. So that's why this meeting in Port Townsend was a very important occasion, because as I said, it meant I was forgiven, and I wanted that. And then he talked to me about how well he had been doing. There was this evidence of his car, and he told me he had two sailboats, and how well he'd been doing in Europe as well as in the United States, and that the money was coming in and coming in. I had a feeling he was saying that my faith in him had been justified. I was very happy for him. He looked great—Eddie Bauer country-gentleman outfit. Remember? His relation to money was a little complicated; he had doubts about enjoying it. He said, "I got this boat and I go out and sit in it and I'm thinking, why the hell am I out on this boat? I should be home writing." *[Laughs.]* Then there were a couple of other things. Apparently now that he had money, certain people were hitting on him. That bothered him . . .

He wrote about that in "Elephant." I felt so good watching you two guys hugging and laughing it up there. Of course, I didn't know all that was going on then.

Well, that's what we talked about. I could see quite clearly enough that he was enjoying himself enormously. He was enjoying life in many ways. He looked very, very good. He had this big car, and he told me about his boats. He was triumphant and his French editor was right there walking around, admiring Ray every minute. All in all, it amounted to a kind of relief for me. I could now with a clear mind and heart pick up the phone and call him any time and talk with him. Not that I hadn't been able to earlier, but there were those little stupid things. I felt happy for him. I'd never stopped loving him. As it happened, some time after that, not too long, I did pick up the phone and call him and heard the horrible news. It wasn't too long after that, was it?

No, that had to be about two months later.

I could hardly talk when he told me what had happened. I choked up, although he was quite sanguine about the whole thing. An operation had been performed. His surgeon told Ray he had read his stories. He loved them. Ray said that there was nothing to worry about; he was all better, out of the woods.

April 4, 1990
Berkeley, California

Ray fishing as a boy.

Vance, Chris, Maryann, and Ray Carver on the island of Rhodes.

WILLIAM KITTREDGE

I remember Ray and me sitting at a bar in Missoula when a woman bartender told us about being arrested the night before, because she and her boyfriend got stoned and moved all their furniture out on the lawn—set up lights and all. After a while, the neighbors got annoyed and called the cops. I looked at Ray and told him that had to be his. So he wrote it—changed it a little.

The interview takes place at the Yarrow Hotel in Park City, Utah, where Kittredge is to give a reading at the Writers At Work conference. I usually find it advisable to chat for a few moments as a warm-up before starting the tape, but I can skip the blather with Bill. He's as comfortable and easy as an old shoe.

We adjourn to the bar after the interview, and he runs off a few stories. I recall talking with him in Aspen on the day we heard that Ray had died. I'll not soon forget the unsentimental, simple manner in which Bill expressed his feelings of loss that day for his dear friend.

Sam Halpert: You and Ray were good friends. When did you first meet him?

William Kittredge: Well, it's real clear. I can be specific because I remember it so vividly. It was during spring break 1970, I was teaching at the University of Montana, and the woman who was my wife at that time and I went to Seattle, you know, just to get out of Montana and hang around for a while at the Olympic, one of the old grand hotels. They were having one of those college English teachers' conventions there, whatever the acronym is. The place was pretty near empty. I don't remember what the meeting was about, but it was something like nine o'clock at night, and they had these long bookstalls with all the publishers' books lined up—maybe two hundred yards of bookstalls and nobody around at all. The place is empty and I'm walking around and looking at these books and trying to resist the impulse to heist a couple of them. My wife and I and a guy way down at the far end were the only ones around. Anyway, I picked up a copy of a book edited by Curt Johnson, who, incidentally, was the publisher of the journal where "Will You Please Be Quiet, Please?" first appeared. I was browsing through the book when this guy walks up. He's kind of a scruffy-looking guy, looks over my shoulder and says, "I've got a story in there." My first impulse was to say something like, "Yeah, I'll bet you have." In any event, we kind of jousted about for a minute or two, and then it turned out it was Ray. I couldn't believe anyone would claim that story if it weren't really theirs. So then we started talking, and he told me he had read a couple stories that I had written, which made him one of the few people in the world I had met that had ever laid eyes on a story of mine. Then we had some coffee and talked some more and someone said, "Let's have a beer," so we went to the bar and someone said, "Let's have a drink." Next thing I know we're just plastered.

I'm glad you remember it so well.

We kind of met as aspiring writers. I was a lot more aspiring than he was, because he had achieved some success by then. But also, we met as drunks, essentially. We were supposed to get together and have dinner the next night, but that didn't work out. I didn't see him again until I got back to Montana. Maybe about a month later I get a letter from this guy and he says he wants to come up and visit. I'm not exactly sure when it was, sometime around in the fall of '70. He and Maryann came from Palo Alto on the train. He came to Montana and I couldn't figure why this guy wanted to do that. I think at this time he felt very isolated.

Why? What was going on in his life at the time?

That was around the year that he stayed home from work for the whole winter and Maryann taught school in Los Altos while he wrote all those stories that were first published in *Esquire,* like "Neighbors" and all those. In those seven or eight months he wrote about twelve stories, all of which were published and all well known today; but he felt really isolated, and I think he was just looking for someone to hang out with—someone to drink with.

How did the visit go?

He came to Missoula, stuck around four or five days, stayed at our house, and met a bunch of the writers there. We had a big time and then he went back. After—I'm not sure of my chronology here, things sort of overlap—by then we were big chums. My ex-wife and I went down to visit him at his house; he was living then in Mountainview. We met Maryann's sister Amy, who is now married to Doug Unger. Again, it was all more big parties. We were roaring along and having high times. There were lots of what we thought of at that time as great adventures. There was this whole system of camaraderie set up.

And how about other visits?

He came back to Missoula and we went back down to visit him. Then in 1972–73 he received a Stegner fellowship at Stanford. The next year I had one, probably in part because Ray put in a good word for me. I went down around June of '73 and, again, more big times. By then the marriage I had was really on the rocks and—

Ray's wasn't doing too well either, I guess.

Well, it came and went in all kinds of ways, but it endured longer than anybody ever thought it would, considering the circumstances.

What happened then?

I went down and stayed with him for a few days, then rented a place and lived there. That was the time Ray was flying back and forth between teaching in Iowa City and Santa Cruz. I and some of his friends would go down and get him off the plane on Thursday afternoon. He'd always come home loaded, and on Friday he was supposed to teach at Santa Cruz. A couple of times he made it, but most of the time we'd pin a note on the door saying "Mr. Carver is too sick to teach"—and it was true. Then he began to not show up at all. Chuck Kinder and I went down once to teach the class together and it was a disaster. I think Ray must have met that class about twice. The provost of the college got wind of what was going on and of Ray also teaching at Iowa City. They fired him, and deservedly so. I don't know what happened to the class and the students. It was a long, dark, hard period for Ray.

How did you and he get along during this period?

When I showed up at Stanford in September '73, the first thing Ray did was take me to a get-together at Chuck Kinder's house and it was one of those fortunate things where there were maybe ten people there and most are still friends of mine. We kept seeing each other in a tight little society of writers and drunks, and we became close friends—dear friends that I have to this day.

This stretch of time sounds very much like what Ray called his "Bad Raymond" days. Could you tell us what you know of how he got out of it?

Well, what happened was we'd visit in San Francisco and see him at Chuck Kinder's place. Chuck had a big, spacious flat, and we'd all gather up there at spring break or Christmas. Ray told me at the time—and I mean there were lots of things I wasn't in on—but the thing that really . . . well, Gordon Lish came to San Francisco to visit on one of those springs and Ray comported himself in a kind of crazy fashion, and I think it was what happened on that visit that compelled him to really look at his life and say, "I have to straighten up or I'm not going to last." It was at this time he made deliberate, life-saving decisions. They weren't very easy decisions. They were difficult; but the narrator in that story "Where I'm Calling From" is closely autobiographical. Ray may have embellished it some, but that was the real stuff.

Did he go to a place to dry out?

Yep. He went to McKinleyville, where he sobered up and where he lived in a little house by himself for a while. He and Maryann were separated at that time, and he told me that what he was doing there mainly was not drinking. He wasn't writing. I remember asking him, after he had been sober for about six months, if he had been writing at all. He said, "I can't. I can't convince myself enough that it is worth doing." That was real shaking to me: "Jesus, this guy's in worse trouble than I thought." Then he slowly found his way back into it, and in a couple of years, of course, he was full steam again. I think those must have been extraordinarily difficult times for him. There was Dick Day—he still teaches up there, I believe—who looked after him a lot while he was drying out in McKinleyville, helped him get through all that stuff.

How did you keep in touch with him after he stopped drinking? Say after '76?

Less and less. We'd write back and forth. Then he went to El Paso, and then Tucson where Tess was teaching. He got a Guggenheim and shortly after that he got the job at Syracuse, and then he and Tess really got together. So it was much less handy to see him. We'd get together maybe once or twice a year. He'd come to Missoula occasionally to give a reading.

Did he seem any different from the old days?

Well, I was sober and I could see this guy trying to look at the world again, and get his ducks in a row, and figure out who he was and how he wanted to comport himself in the world. You could just see him growing, becoming more generous, more open with people, and more reasonable.

Did he ever backslide? Flashes of the old Ray?

Of course there were still elements of his behavior that were eccentric—just being old Ray—but there was always the warmth. But I could see him become more capable in reacting with the world, and the world began to come to him in ways it never did before.

That must have been a hell of an adjustment.

One of the things that interests me, and it's true, is how much he and Dick Hugo were in so many ways alike. They both were guys writing from a kind of disenfranchisement, some sense of not being part of the major world. Writing was a way of justifying your life and celebrating things that didn't seem were properly celebrated. At some point in their careers, they began to be properly recognized. They began to have some success. And I think both of them had trouble for a while with that success, because it was a real change in self-image. They had seen themselves as failures, as people who lived on the margins of things. They both reacted for a while as though saying, "If you think I'm terrific, then watch this."

How do you mean?

Oh, they'd be invited to read at Yale or somewhere, and they'd immediately get drunk for two weeks, as if to deny they were this terrific guy who got invited to Yale. It was, I think, in lots of ways a fear of success, a fear of becoming someone else—someone who negotiated with the world well and easily. And, I think at some point after McKinleyville—some point probably with Tess—Ray turned that corner and realized who he was. He wasn't being false to that other person he once was. He could do all these things and still keep that compassion and generosity. I think the same thing happened to Hugo, but he fell back after a while. When he died, he was drinking heavily again.

That fear of becoming someone else. Lenny Michaels told me about Ray saying that whenever he was out on that boat of his, he couldn't help wondering why the hell he wasn't home writing—where he belonged.

Oh, yes, he could be more ironic than that. He'd look at me once in a while and say, "Are we getting away with it or what?" Something like that. Like, "Look at me, here I am, a guy with a boat!" At the same time, he was very attached to it. He loved having all those things. One of the last times I saw him was in Seattle, almost at the same place where we first met. This was just before he got sick. It was at a celebration for Dick Hugo about November '87. Ray and Tess were staying at a posh hotel near the Market, and Ray was talking about why didn't he and I get together and buy a condo near the Market overlooking the harbor in Seattle and so forth. I don't know where the hell he thought I'd get the money for it, but he was clearly enjoying his success at the time—embracing and having fun with it—on the other hand, not taking it too seriously. He was never obnoxious about it.

But you knew he was enjoying every minute of it?

Oh, yes. Why wouldn't he? After all, he was a saw filer's son from Yakima, and he worked hard, and all these things finally came to him. He got them by himself.

Earlier, you mentioned that "Where I'm Calling From" is largely autobiographical. Of course, that could be said of almost all of Ray's stories, and he received a few knocks for that. Could you comment on that?

I believe every writer discovers the story that's theirs in a way. For a long time, the story that Ray discovered—early on, I think "A Student's Life" was the first one of any consequence—was Ray and Maryann, Ray and Maryann for a long time. One of the things his friends knew and could point out from story to story to story—and Ray was perfectly willing to tell you—was this is the thing that happened, this is where he got that story.

She was not his only source, was she?

No, not the only. I remember Ray and I sitting at a bar in Missoula when a woman bartender told us about being arrested the night before, because she and her boyfriend got stoned and moved all their furniture out on the lawn—set up lights and all. After a while the neighbors got annoyed and called the cops. I looked at Ray and told him that had to be his. So he wrote it—changed it a little. The one about the guy moving all his stuff out in the driveway for a yard sale?

"Shall We Dance?"

Yeah, years later. But mostly he found stories in his life. Then in the transition, when he was quitting the booze, I don't know, because I wasn't with him in the sense of seeing him all the time; I don't know where those stories came from. Like "Cathedral," which I presume came from experiences he and Tess had.

Yes. Tess once worked with a blind man in Seattle.

Seems like it. So he continued to use autobiographical material. I think he had very clear standards that he learned very early on. One of the books I remember in his library in the house in Cupertino was marked up, scribbled all over. It was a college textbook on double stories. You know, Dostoevsky's story "The Double" and that story by Henry James, and all those other doppelganger stories. There was a book he had used in college, maybe in a class with John Gardner. One of the things that struck me about those stories was the way they were like Ray's. Sort of put yourself in my shoes or try my blindness. They were stories that encouraged you to somehow put yourself in someone else's situation imaginatively and thereby generate compassion for them. I believe Ray formed these ideas about storytelling from the very start, way back at Chico State.

You mentioned that small house he lived in when he left McKinleyville. Was that where he got the idea for "Chef's House"?

Must have been. When he left that house, he and Maryann came up to Montana, and we lived in a cabin on Flathead Lake for a week of fishing. Ray was a maniacal fisherman and outfished everybody. He was as singleminded about that as he was about everything else. He was *determined* to catch big fish, and more fish than anybody else, and he did. It was about this time that he and Maryann finally drifted apart. During that week they were amiable, comfortable with each other, but clearly not connected as they had been. Their relationship had broken.

Ray made fictional references to Maryann in many stories and poems, and in his essay in Fires, *he writes openly of the hard years he and Maryann shared. From your perspective, how do you see her affecting his writing?*

Maryann is a person I admired a lot, and I still do, although I think she is to a degree wounded by the things that have happened. But when I knew them, she was the one that kept them together. Ray was the one who stayed home and didn't hold jobs. When I first met him, he was working for SRA in Palo Alto. He soon lost that job and stayed home the next year and wrote, while Maryann worked. She taught school over in Los Altos, and there was an endless kind of chaos surging around them.

But it was a mutual decision. She agreed that Ray should stay home and write, while she worked. She didn't resent that, did she?

Oh, no. She supported him and supported him all the way. She was an extremely intelligent woman. She critiqued his stories. They talked about them. They did interesting things together. They clearly had a mutual agenda, which had to do with his work. She would support him, and that was great. It was a mutual understanding that it would all come to something good, but at the same time it was also somehow very fragile. There was a hell of a lot of drinking going on, and a lot of chaos—unfortunate things during those years—that led to a sense of betrayal on both their parts. It was as though this contract had been fractured and healed up and fractured and healed up, over and over again—so many times that when they finally broke up, Ray told me, "There's been too much water gone under the bridge." I remember his exact words.

Lenny Michaels, in referring to that time, said that they paid for all those stories with their lives.

He's exactly correct. They took risks constantly—risks with their emotional security. They lived on the edge all the time. They stayed out there, and I really think it was a conscious decision on their part to live on those edges, to court experiences.

How would you describe Ray's sentiment about Maryann after their separation, after his "Bad Raymond" days, after he had become successful?

It became difficult for Ray after the separation. He knew he owed her a great debt, and he clearly did in anyone's eyes. She had kept his life together for years and years. She'd helped him imaginatively. They'd been entwined in an emotional compact about getting the work done, and she was clearly portrayed in many of those stories in all kinds of unflattering ways. It didn't bother her at all, at least as far as I could ever tell. It's just so sad that after a long series of emotional betrayals of various kinds, great anger developed. It got so that they couldn't be in the same room together, essentially. Ray felt great sadness, but it made his life impossible to live, impossible to work, impossible for him to do the things he felt he had to do. At the same time, he was so aware of the great debt he owed her. It was a bind for Ray. He knew he had to do his work, but back there all the time was somebody he had left behind.

In one of Ray's later stories, "Intimacy," he depicts a writer who shares many of the feelings you have just described. This fictional writer visits his ex-wife ostensibly to seek forgiveness. How do you view that story?

Of course you never know, but I'd have to say it's a depiction of part of his feelings at least. Ray felt terrific guilt and sorrow, and he felt something valuable had been lost. He also felt that in the nature of their compact, he was the one who had walked away with all the skills—like two people in a contract, and one gets to leave with all the success and the other gets to stand out in the rain. And in a way that is what happened, and Ray felt—as anybody would—great guilt over it. Though I must say I never heard him talk about it in that way; but we both understood it wasn't a thing we *would* talk about.

Is it then possible that "Intimacy" was a sort of payback for Maryann? Perhaps Ray's way of acknowledging his debt to her?

Maybe. It's possible. Of course, you never knew with Ray. In the early days he'd used her so ruthlessly in those stories, and so maybe this was just his way of getting another story. Or maybe it was his way of paying back—probably some of both, for all we know. I don't think it was, "I'm going to make you a gift of this story." Again, I think he took his own guilt, his own life, his own deepest feelings and used them to make art out of it in ways that were partly a payment back to Maryann and at the same time another story.

There's a poem about her in Ray's last book before he died. He seemed to be more generous to her in his poetry than in his fiction.

I've noticed that in his poetry too, at least five or six times.

There's a story there.

I don't know how she feels. I saw her once in Seattle about a year ago. We spoke for about two minutes. It was a strange situation. I was at the University of Washington giving a reading of a piece I had written about Ray after his death. I had no idea she was in the audience. Afterward she came up and she seemed to be very touched and pleased about the piece. We were very friendly for a few minutes, then she just turned and out the door she went. It was the only contact I've had with her in ten years.

Now there's another story. Do you have any favorites among Ray's stories?

Well, "A Small, Good Thing," "Cathedral," maybe the revised version of "Will You Please Be Quiet, Please." I don't know—there are maybe twenty of them, but those are the titles that stand out offhand.

What did you think of his later work?

Well, that story "Intimacy" we were talking about—I don't know; I'm not so sold on that story. I thought "Where I'm Calling From " a great story. I really loved "Errand," about the death of Chekhov. And this may be an aside from your question, but I think Ray was very deliberately changing his art when he died. That's the reason for all those poems. I think that's the reason he was recharging, exploring, looking for new directions. He had explored the old orientation as far as he wanted to. I think he was, as a major artist will, trying to enlarge his scope onto a larger stage. He was feeling his way, and these were all kind of studies toward what he'd begin to do had he not died.

He described how he loved to revise his stories, even those you've mentioned as his best pieces.

I think those longer versions of those stories of his, like "A Small, Good Thing" were really his masterworks. There is a significant difference in the stories as they appeared in *What We Talk About When We Talk About Love* and later versions. For instance, William Abrams, in his introduction to the O. Henry collection in which "A Small, Good Thing" was the leading story, said something like, wasn't it courageous of Ray to take a brief story from his previous book and enlarge it this way? Well, the fact is it was just the opposite. He had written the story, but his editor Gordon Lish had cut it down to the

short version. The short version of that story is enormously dimin-
ished in its emotional power. It's no coincidence that Ray changed
contractual agreements, changed editors and all that. As he told me
afterward, "They can't change a comma from now on."

What's your reaction to all this talk of minimalism?

You know, I took grave exception to, for instance, people like
Madison Smartt Bell attacking Ray for so-called minimalism. It's very
easy to go at somebody's weaker stories and to find fault with them,
which is what I believe Bell's essay did. A writer should be judged on
his best work; that other stuff is forgettable. It's gone and we
shouldn't waste time worrying about it.

Would you say he was not a minimalist?

I don't think of Ray in terms of being minimalist. I don't think he
was an emotional minimalist at all. He was dealing with what was, at
least for me, major emotions. When I reflect and see my own life in
the mirror of some of those great stories, like at the end of "A Small,
Good Thing," these stories are consistently telling me I must learn to
be good, to be humane, compassionate, considerate of other people.
That is a major emotional orientation, and I think it's utterly
important to say, absolutely political. I think Ray had a very sure sense
of his politics. He was simply saying we have to be more compassionate,
we have to be more considerate of each other. Ray said that over and
over again in major ways in all those stories.

June 14, 1990
Park City, Utah

ROBERT STONE

He represents in a way a renewal of the American realist tradition . . . an inheritor of Hemingway, an inheritor of Sherwood Anderson. . . . People will always want to read him to get an insight into the life and art of late twentieth-century America.

This interview was held at the Rebel's Roost, a nineteenth-century guest house maintained by Sewanee University for visiting writers and lecturers. Stone was a guest there while running a two-week fiction workshop at the Sewanee Writers' Conference.

He did not express much enthusiasm when approached for the interview. He'd been interrogated countless times for book reviews and literary journals. He claimed he had nothing new to say, and every minute of his time at the conference had been spoken for. His card was full. Then, perhaps because he is basically a kind man, he thought he could squeeze me in Saturday morning, the last day of the conference, at nine. It was early in the morning for both of us.

Sam Halpert: Where did you first meet Ray?

Robert Stone: I believe we first met in California some time in the sixties—or to put it another way, we were at the same party in San Francisco. I'd see him on odd occasions after that, but the first time I really got to know him was in Toronto at the Harbor Literary Festival they have every year. That was sometime in the eighties. We got to talk—much more than people usually do at such conferences. I told him how much I admired his work. As I recall, this took place at a historic restaurant, sort of a Williamsburg restoration that they took us to.

After that . . .

After that I saw him at his house in Port Angeles a couple of times. We went fishing together. He had a boat. One year when we were fishing, we got lost in the fog. We had a really good time. Ray had a manner that was very much his own, a kind of shambling and colorful manner of viewing things. There was something incongruous about him out there in his boat. We caught a lot of salmon and had a very good time. I don't remember much else that happened that particular time. I was staying with him.

I remember Tess and I drinking some great single-malt Scotch, I drinking most of it. Raymond had been on the wagon for years and years. Funny, that's all I remember from that time, the boat and the single-malt Scotch.

That boat. Lenny Michaels remembers Ray wondering just what the hell he was doing out on that boat when he could be home writing. Did you recognize that?

Yes. He had a relationship with the boat that was always ambiguous, and Raymond was the master of ambiguity.

Ambiguity? Ray Carver?

Well, highly impacted. Ambiguous in the sense that you don't always know exactly what a character is feeling. Or to put it in another way—his characters give you the impression of experiencing a number of different things at one time. I think you can call that ambiguity.

You mentioned that Ray was on the wagon, but we know he wrote many fine stories before he gave up alcohol. How do you think that affected his writing?

Well, all I know is that he thought it did. I know being an alcoholic is a great disrupter of energy, and he wrote with a great burst of energy after he stopped drinking. Anyway, that's what he used to say. I don't know where the cut-off point is in terms of his stories. I know it must have made a difference. He believed it did.

Was it Cheever who said he could always detect a line written by a drinking author? Something like that. Could Carver or any writer turn out good stuff while drinking?

I don't know. It's not possible for me to write while intoxicated. There are people who do it. I mean, it's not like it hasn't been done.

Fitzgerald, according to what we read, wrote with a bottle. I don't think it's terribly uncommon, but in terms of a short story I can't do it.

You had read Carver before you met him?

Oh, yes, I had read some of his stories before, but more after I had met him.

What difference do you see between the stories he wrote before he stopped drinking compared to the ones he wrote afterward?

I'm afraid I can't tell you much about that. I'm not too familiar with when he wrote what, so I couldn't say which of his stories he wrote before he stopped drinking.

Let's try something else. Which of his stories do you consider most characteristically Carver?

Yes, the one where the guy occupies his neighbor's apartment while he's gone on a trip. I believe it's called "Neighbors." I loved that story. I think that so represents Carver.

What's your opinion of his last story, "Errand"?

It was quite different—like he was about to to enter a whole new phase. I understand that Tess found many stories in his files after he was gone.

When I asked Tobias Wolff which story he considered most characteristically Carver's, he cited a poem called "The Baker." What do you think of Carver's poetry?

I like it very much. I think Raymond was working toward a kind of refining of his vision, and as his stories became more and more accomplished, he began to compress even more. He found certain things that he was expressing so succinctly that they became poetry.

In the last few months of his life, he wrote no stories, only poetry. What was your sense of that?

I admired his poetry very much. I think he was going to be—he *is*— a major American poet.

In your estimation, where do you believe Carver's work will stand in American literature?

I think his work will stand very high. He represents in a way a renewal of the American realist tradition. He is an inheritor of Hemingway, an inheritor of Sherwood Anderson. His work is very good and very rewarding. People will always want to read him to get an insight into the life and art of late twentieth-century America. He has an international reputation. I think he will stand high.

Carver's experience and life seems to be in every page he wrote. As his friend, as well as fellow writer, could you comment on that?

To a certain extent his life and work did combine. I had a great affection for Carver. While we lived on opposite sides of the country, we were friends. He had personal qualities that were reflected in his work—a certain kind of excellence, generosity, perceptiveness. He cared about people. His writing was very much the way he was. You could admire and love the man in the same way you could love and admire the writing.

That recalls the passage in Catcher In The Rye *where Holden Caulfield talks about books that when you finish reading you wish the author was a terrific friend and you could phone him whenever you felt like it.*

Something like that. Sometimes you'd meet the man and it would be disappointing, but in the case of Carver it wouldn't be.

His poem, "My Boat," conveys that open spirit and friendship to one and all.

The man was very much like his work.

Can you recall the circumstance where you first heard of his fatal illness?

I had heard from others that he was ill. Then one night I was standing behind him at the Literary Lions night at the New York Public Library where everyone dresses up in a tuxedo. I slapped him on the back, and when he turned around I could see he had lost an enormous amount of weight. That's when I saw that he was really very ill. I remember being very alarmed and shocked at the way he looked.

It is tragic that there will never be another Carver story.

It's a great loss—the premature death of an artist of such stature. A great loss.

July 28, 1990
Sewanee, Tennessee

Ray Carver, Doug Unger,
Amy Burk Unger on
Christmas Eve 1987 at
Stephen Dobyns' home in
Syracuse. The photo was a
Christmas present from Ray.

JAY MCINERNEY

I think Ray was much too modest to realize how widespread an influence he was. I mean, you look at all the short-story writers younger than Ray, and there's hardly one that, you might say, didn't come out of Carver's overcoat. I'm sure Ray was not aware how influential he was.

When I asked McInerney for the interview, he readily agreed, no questions asked. As I recall, his reply was something like—if it's for Ray, I'm for it. We set up an appointment easily, with no jockeying around. It took place in the living room of his recently remodeled Greenwich Village house four days after I first phoned him. I tell him that I believe "Raymond Carver: A Still, Small Voice" [*New York Times Book Review*, August 6, 1989], the memoir of his days at Syracuse with Ray, was one fine piece of writing. He is glad that the piece has been so well received, as Ray had been such a positive force in his life.

Sam Halpert: Did you meet Ray before you were his student at Syracuse?

Jay McInerney: I first met him here in New York. Oddly enough, I opened the door of my apartment in Greenwich Village, and standing there was Raymond Carver, who at that time was my favorite writer. It wasn't quite as coincidental and weird as that. In fact, my friend Gary Fisketjon, my current editor, was working at that time as an editor at Random House. Gary was a friend of Gordon Lish, who worked at Knopf. Well, one day Ray Carver came to town to give a reading at Columbia, and Gary and Gordon had lunch with Carver. After lunch they both had meetings and work to attend to, and Ray didn't really have much to do. So Gary called me up and asked me if I could take Ray around and maybe show him the city.

Had you been published at that time?

No. I knew Gary from Williams where we had become best friends. He was just starting out as an editor at that time. So he called me up—this was actually the day that John Lennon died.

That would make it in the winter of 1980?

Yes, around that. Gary asked me if I wanted to meet Carver. I thought he was kidding and I hung up on him. He called me back and said, "No, seriously, Carver is coming to your house." And within moments there was a knock on my door, and there was this giant bear of a man in my doorframe. I recognized him at once as Carver and welcomed him in. The idea, I guess, was that I should take him sightseeing or something, occupy him for four or five hours' time.

And how did you do that?

Well, we just sat down and started talking about one thing or another, mainly about books and writing, and we never got out of the apartment. The time just flew. Then Richard Ford came by. He was a friend of Ray's. It was the first time I had met him. We all had a wonderful time talking, and the next thing we knew it was time for Ray's reading at Columbia, and Gary came to pick him up.

How did you follow this up?

After that I wrote Ray a letter telling him how happy I was to meet him. I was surprised when he wrote me right back. We started a correspondence and subsequently when he came to New York, he'd visit with me and Gary. We started to become friends.

Were you working on your novel at that time?

At that time I was working on a novel that I never finished, and some short stories. When I met Ray I was just basically trying to support myself as a freelance writer doing research writing and book reviews. It wasn't easy. That was one of the things Ray recognized when we corresponded.

What was that?

He said if I really wanted to make it as a serious writer—commit myself to the act of writing fiction—I would have to arrange my life accordingly. He felt that living in New York and having to support myself in the most expensive city in the country was draining away a lot of my energy. After about a year of this I was just numb. He suggested I consider coming up to Syracuse to study with him.

Why do you believe he did that?

Well, there were two aspects to his interest in having me come up there—one being that he felt that my devoting two years to learning how to write fiction was a good idea. And he felt New York was a crazy place for me.

He wasn't too far off there.

No, he wasn't. I'm still amazed he took the time to encourage me, because I had some resistance. I still felt I was in the center of the media and publishing world. Sometimes it's easy to confuse that with, you know, the literary world. The literary world exists wherever there are writers, and wherever there is a man or a woman alone in a room writing. That's the literary world, and I was a little foolish in confusing the one thing with the other.

How did you settle that confusion?

Carver nudged me along with the idea of graduate school. For me the idea of graduate school didn't make much sense unless I would study with a writer I greatly admired. To me Carver was the best writer going, so I applied for graduate school and received a fellowship, which enabled me more or less to afford to live.

Ray must have been behind that.

I imagine he had a lot to do with that, and subsequently he helped me find an apartment; so in the fall of '79 I moved up to Syracuse, about a half block away from Ray and not too far away from Tobias Wolff.

Did you work with Wolff too?

I worked with Toby, too. Toby is a great teacher. It was remarkable—for a brief time we had a wonderful little community. Ray was instrumental in bringing Toby to Syracuse. He attracted many good people—Tess Gallagher, Doug Unger, Hayden Carruth—

How did you do up there?

I think what Ray did for me really changed my life. I think it's quite possible that if I hadn't met Ray, I would have gone down the wrong road. I'd be an editor of a magazine today, or something like that—which is not to say there's anything dishonorable with that; but one thing Ray did for me was to pound away at the idea that the only way to be a good writer was to write every day. Sometimes he'd even call me up, if he hadn't seen me, and ask, "Did you write today?"

Did he follow his own advice?

I remember many years later as a joke calling him to ask if he'd written that day, and he said, "No, you have to write every day until you *are* a writer; then you can take a day off every now and then."

So do you now take a day off every now and then?

[Laughs.] I take days off. On the other hand, Ray was the first one to teach me that writing well is a lot of hard work and you can't be afraid to sit down every day and pound away at it. Even if, and especially if, it is not coming well.

Did you work with others at Syracuse?

I was enrolled in the program. I guess it was for an M.A., but my primary interest was to study with Ray and to have time to write. Everything else was a bit of an annoyance. But I also had the added bonus of Tobias Wolff who was an excellent teacher, an important writer, a good squash player, and a great guy there as well.

Was Ray your primary influence?

Both men were very important to my development, but I suppose

Ray was my mentor. Long before I'd met him, his work had inspired me. Subsequently he did spend a lot of time with me. I could always bring him a story. He'd go over it with me.

Even if you weren't enrolled in a class of his?

Yes. That was the nice thing about it. I think Ray felt the same way. The whole classroom structure was an annoyance to him, too. He didn't particularly like teaching, standing up in front of a class. He was a very modest man.

How was he one on one?

Oh, when he'd take a manuscript and red-pencil it, there's no doubt he had authority. He could always take a story and make it better. He was an excellent line editor. He was a great coaxer of stories—whatever was there that was any good, he would find it.

How would he treat a bad story?

He was never harsh. His criticisms were roundabout. The worst thing Ray would say about a story was, "I'm glad you got that behind you." What he meant by that was there was no further point writing the ninth draft of that story. Eight was enough to get it out of your system, and you didn't have to go back to it anymore. He was willing to indulge you and that was about the harshest thing I ever heard him say.

How else did he motivate you?

He was also my mentor in the sense that he was the first writer who encouraged me—made me feel I had talent. I looked up to him. I wanted to be, somehow, a writer in the same way that he was a writer. I wanted to learn by example.

Did you?

You know, I'd thought that writing was something that took place between drinking bouts, or travels to exotic lands, or between your seventh and eighth marriage. That was certainly one prominent model of the writer in America. Ray taught me the real job was sitting down every day and, as he said, putting black on white. That was very inspiring.

What more did you learn from him?

Well, you know, he'd been through so much by the time I met him, and he'd come out the other side. He insisted that what he'd been through had only distracted him from writing. I think his writing improved as he sobered up, so he was also a steadying influence on my life in giving me a model of the writer that wasn't a self-destructing meteor.

Like . . . ?

Let's face it: like most of the more conspicuous American writers were and are.

Getting back to Ray. You said that you saw him as not very comfortable in the role of teacher . . .

Ray was somewhat an unwilling teacher. That is to say, he was so modest he almost didn't trust himself to give advice. I think he believed it a peculiar fate that led him to be a teacher. He thought it strange that so many American writers supported themselves by teaching. On the other hand, he thought it was better than sweeping floors or pumping gas, which he had done in the past.

Those who were close to him have commented that he regarded his success as an unexpected gift, as if he was getting away with something. Did you notice that?

That was an endearing trait of Ray's. Right up to the very end, he seemed flabbergasted by each new honor. I remember he once called me to tell me that the *New York Times* was going to do a profile on him. He said, "Can you believe it? The *New York Times!*" Well, of course I believed it. Anybody would. I changed my whole life to follow him to Syracuse—hardly at the top of my list of favorite places to live if Ray wasn't there. He was considered one of our greatest writers, but he was constantly amazed at the high regard in which people held his work.

You've said that you have high regard for his stories. But beyond that, what do you see in his work?

One of the things that hasn't been mentioned enough is that each of his major collections represented a different stage in his development. That was not frequently noticed. People kept discovering him, as if he'd just been born. That is to say, even the *New York Times* review of his second book, *What We Talk About When We Talk About Love,* was actually a review of his first book. And so we were disappointed that the reviewer treated it all as one lump.

This collection—What We Talk About When We Talk About Love—*wasn't this the one where the stories seem pared down to a bare minimum?*

Yes, this was the collection that fixed a stereotyped image of minimalism to his work. The collection went very far in exploring how much can be left out in a story—the old Hemingway notion. In fact, so much was left out that Ray subsequently published these stories in their original and, to me, more satisfying longer versions.

Do you find his earlier work preferable to his later?

I wouldn't pick one period over another. To me it's remarkable to see the continuity *and* the development. That is to say, by the time Ray published his first book, he knew what he was doing. I suppose nothing could have the impact on me that "Will You Please Be Quiet, Please?" did, because it was like a bolt out of the blue. For some of us it must have been like picking up *In Our Time* for the first time—suddenly this very new language, this wonderful new idiom. It's the world as you always suspected, but you never realized it was, until you read the book. It had an incredible impact, and I suppose I'll always love that book, especially as it hit me so hard.

Which of his stories would you call typical of his early work?

One of the earlier stories typifies some of the ways Ray felt about fiction. "Put Yourself in My Shoes," is very much what Ray said fiction is all about. It was the first story I heard him read at Columbia on the night that I met him. When I first read the story, I felt the menace in it. Like much of his work, it has an edge of darkness. But when I heard Ray read it, what came through was the humor. The effect his reading had on the audience was remarkable. It was remarkable in the way you felt impelled to laugh at some of the most awkward moments. I think he liked that and thought it was not an inappropriate response to his work.

Which of his later stories would you single out?

So many people discovered Carver in his later work like "Cathedral." It's an interesting story for me because I heard him tell it so many times before he wrote it down. It was fascinating to see it develop. The first time I went to Syracuse, I stayed with Ray and Tess. Ray told me of the visit of the blind friend of Tess's. It was a very funny story. At the time I didn't hear anything of the cathedral or the television show. It was just a series of funny stories that Ray was telling on himself about his own discomfort having to be around this blind man. Ray was a quirky guy, full of idiosyncrasies that all his friends could mimic. He made fun of them himself, both on and off the page.

What did you think of "Cathedral" when you read the book?

Something remarkable happens in that story that usually doesn't happen in a Carver story. It has a different kind of ending. The ending of a usual Carver story leaves you on the brink of an abyss, and you look down into it. In "Cathedral" it's more like you're looking up to the sky and the sun is coming out. It's an unusual story for Ray in many ways, and I think he was proud of it for that reason.

It is an unusual Carver story. Where did you see a difference besides the ending?

In "Cathedral," as well as in "A Small, Good Thing" there was perhaps a new emphasis, a compassion for how we have to deal with each other—which is not to say the stories are better or worse. Ray was sensitive to the charge of middlebrow critics that his work was consistently depressing. In "Cathedral" he was saying that, although life is tragic, perhaps once in a while you can beat the odds.

As you say, Ray received his share of adverse criticism, and you are certainly no stranger to the form. Would you care to comment about bad reviews?

Well, I wouldn't want to equate Ray's with my rap. I think he did take a few bad raps. One of the things I learned from reading Ray's critics, and knowing his work as I did, is how often even our best literature is caricatured, and how even a writer as widely admired as Ray is so often misunderstood, even when he is being praised. He got a lot of satisfaction from his press, although he was often bewildered when he read about himself. I guess ultimately he thought, "Well, okay, if it's good we'll take it to the bank and not worry too much about it." But this minimalist thing always bothered him. Ray wrote the way that he wrote, and he felt it was a belittling term. He didn't believe his work was any more minimalistic than anyone else's. I remember three bad reviews that Ray received and he never forgot them.

Could you tell us?

I don't want any names here because these people are still around. I told Ray I'd get them sooner or later. *[Laughter.]* Naaah, by getting them I mean to say that some day I would let it be known that the reviews were wrong and spiteful. I'm saying that it's altogether too easy for critics to forget that there's a person at the other end of the work. I did see Ray hurt by a few reviews, but on the other hand I don't think many writers have been as highly regarded and appreciated in his lifetime as was Ray. Overall, I'd say it was a joy to see so good a writer so well appreciated. On balance I'd say that Ray felt he was really blessed, and he was blessed—even though some of us felt frustrated by what we considered to be the awkwardness and stupidities of some of the more casual criticism.

When I queried Toby Wolff about this, he said something to the effect that perhaps we should all be so lucky as to be considered the head of the column to be attacked.

[Laughs.] Well, Ray was such an unlikely leader. I think Ray was much too modest to realize how widespread an influence he was. I

mean, you look at all the short-story writers younger than Ray, and there's hardly one that, you might say, didn't come out of Carver's overcoat. I'm sure Ray was not aware how influential he was. One year I was a reader for an anthology of short stories put out by Random House, called the *Random Review,* which didn't last very long. I had to read all the literary magazines to pick out the year's best, and that was the year when just about every story in those literary magazines was an imitation of a Carver story. It was astonishing how many people were trying to write like him, myself included.

His work seems so simple until you sit down and try to do it.

It's impossible to do it the way he did it. The best you can do is learn from it and develop your own voice and style from it, as so many have who started out as Carver disciples. There's an extended family of writers who were so touched by his work that they feel like they were his friends.

August 17, 1990
New York, New York

DOUGLAS UNGER

Maryann had heard of a place called Duffy's, an alcoholic rehabilitation center in Myrtledale, California. Duffy's is the model for Frank Martin's place in "Where I'm Calling From." Ray had nowhere to go. He had no money, couldn't pay the rent.

Unger welcomes me on the front porch of the small house that he and his wife, Amy, occupy just off the Syracuse campus. She asks me whether I intend to interview her sister, Maryann Carver. I'd been strongly considering that possibility since the Michaels and Kittredge interviews, but neither of them had any idea where she might be, nor if she'd be willing to participate in an interview. She'd never spoken to anyone for publication. Amy offers to help me take care of that little problem.

It's a quiet Saturday summer afternoon in Syracuse. Quiet, but for the clatter of a neighbor mowing his lawn. Doug and I go inside for the interview. He offers me a cold beer. Two guys in shirtsleeves, sitting at a dining room table and talking into a small tape recorder. They smile from time to time. The bright afternoon sun recedes behind the neighbor's house, casting long shadows across the table. The mowing stops. The guys keep on. They are having a serious talk.

Sam Halpert: Do you remember how you first met Ray?

Douglas Unger: I like to think back to the first occasion that I met Ray through his writing, much before I actually met Ray Carver the man. It was when I was the managing editor of the *Chicago Review* and the story "They're Not Your Husband" came into the office—

What year was this?

The fall of '73. And the way I discovered Ray's work was the unusual way that manuscript came to the office. In those days we were generally getting piles of submissions every month through the mail, really more than we could read seriously. But this story came in hand-carried by the editor, Richard Hack. He had just been given the story by Curt Johnson of December Press, who I believe had the story passed on to him at a writers' conference in Wisconsin. So I had the impression that Ray Carver stories were being passed on like that, in a kind of wonderful underground way, all around the country. We read that story with excitement, right away, that minute, because it came to us like that, and we discovered that "They're Not Your Husband" seemed to be something entirely new in those days.

New? In what way new?

Back then, in the early seventies, the editorial focus and the majority of the manuscripts we were reading seemed to be of a kind of so-called experimental fiction that Ray later often spoke out against: highly textured prose, with highly innovative and surreal subjects—a fiction called metafiction, as in the styles of Pynchon and Coover, and Barth and Barthelme and Hawkes—writers who were very much in vogue then. "They're Not Your Husband" was nothing like that. It was a straightforward story, realistic, with an unadorned style that also had a lot of humor in its implications. There was also a very strange dark quality to the writing that I felt myself immediately drawn to. As I remember it, Richard Hack and I and some of the staff decided to accept the story that same day. We had never acted that quickly before. That was my introduction to Ray's writing. I had no way of knowing that later I'd not only meet the man but also become part of his family.

How did you follow up your early interest in his work?

I heard a lot about Ray, and read as many of his stories as I could find, when I was at the Iowa Workshop. There were all kinds of tales about him. Let's just say that he had cut a swath in Iowa City. But the students all loved him and couldn't praise him enough. He and John Cheever had been famously drunk together in Iowa City on many an occasion, and the workshop was still recovering.

Cheever and Carver—their names go together—right out of Dickens. Did they in fact get along?

Ray admired John Cheever's writing. And I know they became fast friends almost immediately, and it was a great literary friendship.

52

What was Ray's status as a writer at that time?

By the time Ray arrived at Iowa, he'd been writing serious fiction for at least fourteen years. He'd been published in many fine literary journals. He had received prizes and was anthologized—*The Best Short Stories of '67, The Best Little Magazine Fiction of '71 and '72,* and in the O. Henry award stories. He had, at that point, two stories published or accepted by Gordon Lish at *Esquire.* But he'd reached a kind of ending point both in his life and his writing. He was perhaps at one of the lowest points in his life, and he was still sinking.

What was the main problem?

A good part of the problem was money. He was terribly broke and had declared bankruptcy. In those days Ray often used to say, "I never had a problem that money couldn't solve." But I think a bigger problem was that no publisher anywhere in the country would accept his book, *Will You Please Be Quiet, Please?* The collection represented fourteen years of work. Still, editors found the stories too depressing, or not in tune with what the culture wanted to read, and the book wouldn't sell. Short-story collections were very hard to get published back then. For one reason or another he was turned down, time and again. The way he came to teach in Iowa—

Was that his first time at Iowa?

No, he had been a student there before. Most people aren't aware that Ray had been a student in poetry at the Iowa Writers' Workshop when Paul Engle was the director in '63 and '64. And Engel didn't renew Ray's financial aid. Ray was so shy back then. He'd had poems published, and at least one long story called "Furious Seasons," which he had used as part of his application to Iowa. But he wasn't the kind to show off his work easily. He was very quiet in the workshops. Engle hadn't noticed him or his work and didn't renew Ray's financial aid for the second year.

Ray was married and had two young children and responsibilities. You get a picture of all this in his essay "Fires," in the description of running the laundry through—at the mercy of the "law of the laundromat," he calls it—and of his terrible frustration, wishing for writing time and feeling that his life is a small, change thing. One thing that's not said in "Fires" is how good a father Ray was then. He took care of the kids a lot. His wife, Maryann, worked as a full-time waitress at the Athletic Club to pay the bills. Not getting aid was a crushing blow.

After all that, how did he come to teach at Iowa?

That's a kind of sad story. He had sent "Will You Please Be Quiet, Please?" in to the Iowa Short Fiction Award contest. Even though the preliminary judges selected his book to win, for some reason their decision was reversed and it didn't win. Jack Leggett, who was director of the workshop, was outraged at that decision. He was so outraged that he told everyone that not only did he think that Ray's manuscript should have won first prize hands down but that he was going to offer Ray a teaching job. So he invited Ray to teach the following year.

Then how did you finally get to meet Ray?

I met Ray through my wife, Amy, three months after I met her. Ray's wife then, Maryann, is Amy's sister. I fell in love with Amy at Iowa in the fall of '75, when I was a teaching fellow at the workshop, and she was finishing her M.F.A. in acting. Ray's name began to come up, and I began hearing a lot of the family stories about him—especially how concerned Amy was for her sister Maryann, and the volatility of her marriage with Ray at that time. Amy was concerned about their children, too. Life was hard for all of them, because of the then-raging alcoholism, the continual rejections, and the constant financial problem.

You didn't know Amy was Ray's sister-in-law when you met her?

No; after we met we might have had a talk or two about it. Amy got regular phone calls from Ray and Maryann. But we were too busy just being in love those first few weeks. Then it came up that we were invited to Ray and Maryann's home in Cupertino for Christmas that year. The whole San Francisco and Stanford writers' scene were there. I met Bill Kittredge there for the first time, and Chuck Kinder and Jim Crumley.

There are quite a few stories about those Cupertino parties . . .

Sometimes you might find just about every important writer from the Rockies to the West Coast and down to Santa Barbara. Lenny Michaels would be there, and Tomás Sanchez, Max Crawford, Chuck Kinder, Bill Kittredge, maybe Gurney Norman and Ed McClanahan. It was a famous scene. Those parties would go on for weeks sometimes, moving from one place to another. The day I first met Ray was at the beginning of a long holiday party like that. I flew in ahead of Amy because of airplane ticket deals. Ray met me at the airport in a broken-down Mercury Comet station wagon full of dents and rattles and barely running. He looked like a man at the edge of death from drinking.

What year are we in?

This is December '75. Ray was waiting at the airport and he had the shakes. He could hardly wait to retrieve the bags, so he could get back to the car and reach under the seat for his bottle of vodka. Then we drove up to Chuck and Diane Kinder's apartment in San Francisco and the party began. That whole Christmas was one long crazy party.

Were you meeting Maryann for the first time, too?

Yes, Amy and I stayed at their home in Cupertino. It was a fun time. It was also a very rough holiday because of all the drinking. Yet Ray was so funny about that, too. As soon as he got up in the morning, everyone in the house had to get up to keep him company. He'd knock on the door and shout, "Hot doughnuts! Steaming hot coffee! Come on! How about a little heart starter? Let's all just have a heart starter here!" And he'd have Bloody Marys and coffee and doughnuts along with plates of food out on the table. He'd get everybody up. We'd all tie into our drinks and be off and running again. It was a wild time.

Did you get a chance to talk to him about writing while all this was going on?

I talked to him some about writing. But writing was the last thing he wanted to talk about with a young writer from Iowa. I think he met

55

me fully expecting to dislike me and any of the academic *chi-chi* he thought I represented.

Did he consider you an upstart?

No, but I think he expected me to be an upstart. And don't forget I was a young guy invading his home, in love with his sister-in-law, whom he loved a great deal. But we actually grew very close over the holidays. I met his brother, James, and his mother, Ella, and his children, Chris and Vance. It was a good Christmas for the kids, generally. Ray played Santa Claus. Amy's daughter—our daughter—Erin, called him Uncle Ray, too. Along with all the good times, I later helped Ray intervene in a difficult family situation that involved his daughter. And he stood up for me in a drunken fight, in his living room, with one of Amy's former boyfriends. We spent three weeks together, all of us partying hard, or just telling stories and jokes and mainly laughing. It was a rough time but it was also a very good time. We simply lived through so much together that by the end of the holiday we were close friends.

Do you remember what you and Ray talked about mostly?

We talked about people. His friends. Family matters. Day-to-day things. And we talked a lot about books. He only talked a little bit about his own writing. At that time he had the galleys of *Will You Please Be Quiet, Please?* Gordon Lish had gone from *Esquire* to McGraw-Hill, and I believe one of the conditions of his accepting the job as editor was that he would bring Ray's book with him and publish it there. So Ray did have that book finally on its way to being published. But to him, I think he
felt this was happening way too late.

You'd think he'd be elated. What was the problem?

He was proud of the book, sure; but in a lot of ways he was also very, very grim. I remember his house in Cupertino had a lemon tree out back that was profuse with fruit that no one ever picked or tended. And Ray's study was like that tree; books and manuscripts and papers piled up and collecting dust. He hadn't been able to work for a long time. There was so much chaos and turmoil going on in his personal life, fueled by all the drinking, that it was impossible for him to go on.

How did they manage? Who paid the bills?

Maryann was teaching English at the high school in Los Altos, where she had worked for eight years. She had always worked. More than Ray, she paid the bills and supported the family and did everything else. But ends just didn't meet in that house. Ray at that point was hanging paper all over town, writing hot checks just to get enough liquor to get through the day.

Did he go into bankruptcy? He often wrote about it.

This was his second bankruptcy. Those stories are based on actual incidents that happened to him. In fact, I can think of only two or three stories he wrote that were not in some way based on incidents in his own life or in his own family.

Which are . . . ?

One is "The Train," which is a continuation of and a homage to a John Cheever story. Another is "Errand," his last story. But generally, I think his stories have, at their core, and as points of departure, actual incidents he came across in his life.

Well, there's his story "The Pheasant." It's hard to see Ray in that story of a Hollywood bit actor, a sort of gigolo, in that car with the aging actress. Where did he get that?

He used things from everyone, things that he heard. Amy was an actress, a pro who had been on Broadway, and told him many stories. In fact, during this whole Christmas party it was amazing to me as a young writer to sit at the table with Bill Kittredge and Ray and Chuck Kinder and the others and hear them telling stories on each other and topping each other. Ray would ask, "Are you going to use that one? Because if you're not, it's mine." And they all went around the table that way.

But Ray wasn't writing at that time?

No, but he still told great stories. The not working and all the drinking and the holidays were very hard on Ray and Maryann financially and every other way. Toward the end of Christmas it was like a burnout, especially for Maryann, who had to be back at her job, paying bills and putting food on the table. Ray was in very bad shape by then.

But he did pull out of it somehow. A year later he stopped drinking. Could you tell us how he managed to pull out of it?

Well, Amy and I were a part of that, in for the long haul. Ray came to Iowa City that spring. There was continuing strife in his marriage: they were going to separate; then they were going to stay together; they were going to split up again. A lot of it is shown in the stories in *What We Talk About When We Talk About Love*—the infidelity committed by the man that destroys trust, followed by all the guilt and heavy drinking—stories such as "Gazebo" and "A Serious Talk" and "One More Thing." That was just about exactly what was going on in his life. That spring, he came to Iowa City to give a reading. He was supposed to be on his way to Yaddo after that, but he got drunk the day of the reading and stayed so drunk he never made it out of town. He lived at our house in Iowa City for about two months. Then he went back to San Francisco to rejoin Maryann and try to work through the problem.

How did that work out?

It was a rough time for everyone. We also moved to San Francisco that summer. That was when Ray began his rounds to attempt to quit drinking once and for all.

How long did that last?

He started to try to stop drinking from the summer of '76 through the fall and into '77. He had an apartment in San Francisco at first, and when he gave that up he would stay with us or with Chuck and Diane Kinder, who had a big apartment across the street. In between he would go back to live with Maryann. Amy and I rented our flat from the St. James Episcopal Church, where meetings of Alcoholics Anonymous were held. Maryann was the most influential in trying to help. She had sobered up first and was very serious about a twelve-step program. She was willing to do anything to save Ray. We all knew he was going to die if he didn't quit drinking. And he knew it, too.

That was a grim time.

What happened next was he was affected by CNS seizures.

CNS seizures?

For a certain number of alcoholics, especially the heaviest drinkers, their nervous system has become so adjusted to having alcohol that when they stop drinking they go into seizures, as though with epilepsy. These seizures are very dangerous. It's how brains are damaged during convulsions.

It's like "Where I'm Calling From."

Yes. Ray had hit the floor several times, like the character Tiny in that story. That's where the detail is from. Ray was the one who was on the floor with his heels clicking. He was then terrified to quit drinking, because it had happened in a hospital in San Francisco and it had happened when he'd tried to quit on his own; so he kept on drinking. He and Maryann split up again. Ray began a relationship with another woman who, as in "Where I'm Calling From," was shortly after diagnosed as having cancer. That story is almost entirely taken from his life at that time.

But he did eventually stop?

As I said, he made so many attempts over that year and a half to stop drinking. Many of us were trying to help him. Once I accompanied Chuck Kinder and Ray to a summer home up in Tiburon, loaned to us for that purpose. Chuck and Ray were going to try to stop drinking together. But they weren't there four hours before they discovered a fully stocked liquor cabinet, and the whole thing turned into a kind of drinking contest between them.

Before that, Ray had rented a small apartment on Castro Street in San Francisco. Just like in "Careful," which describes that apartment exactly, Ray had somehow convinced himself that if he only drank champagne, he'd be able to taper off and quit. He'd go out in the morning and buy bottles of the cheapest Andre, but this wasn't working and he knew it. At that point, everyone had given up hope.

We all thought he would keep on drinking until it killed him. And he thought so, too.

How did he come out of that? What made him turn around?

As with so many important events in his life, it was Maryann. She had heard of a place called Duffy's, an alcoholic rehabilitation center in Myrtledale, California. She was selling the house in Cupertino and had scraped together the money for a rehab center for Ray. This place, Duffy's, is the model for Frank Martin's in "Where I'm Calling From." Ray had nowhere else to go. He had no money, couldn't pay the rent. He was so desperate for money that he took a job as clerk in the Tides bookstore in Sausalito, but he didn't stay there for more than a couple of weeks. His hunger for books ate up much of his salary. He never stopped reading, no matter how much he drank, and he'd bring home armloads of books. He quit that job and then hit rock bottom.

Maryann offered him the chance to go to Duffy's to dry out—almost the last chance to save his life. So she and Amy and I drove Ray up to Duffy's. And he was terrified. Terrified that he was going to die if he stopped drinking, or end up brain-damaged from the seizures, the convulsions.

What a bind! Dead if you do and dead if you don't.

The doctors had given him six months and he'd be dead—maybe sooner. I remember, when we checked him in at Duffy's, he was dead drunk. He'd been drinking all the way up as we drove through the Napa Valley; but after that first experience at Duffy's, we saw the turn begin to happen. He was there for about three weeks the first time. Then he got out of Duffy's—

He checked himself out of Duffy's?

As I remember it, he checked himself out, concerned about the money it cost, and also believing that he had learned enough about the disease of alcoholism that he could quit now. He went back and lived with Maryann for a brief period. That didn't work out, so he came to live with us. He didn't last long without a drink that first time. The personal and family problems and the social pressure to drink—all his old buddies in San Francisco—it was just too much for him. He felt a desperate sadness over the breakup of his marriage. And the children were in trouble, too. His daughter, in particular, was in deep trouble. I don't want to go into the details, but she's doing just fine now, and she has three beautiful daughters of her own.

What about his son?

Vance wasn't in any kind of physical trouble. But, of course, he was very emotionally wounded by the tremendous disarray in their lives. I had a great deal of sympathy for Chris and Vance, and I still do. Vance was really caught between. He had to finish high school, his parents were alcoholics, and his home had been yanked out from under him. He was a physically big young man, like his Dad, and at times became violent with Maryann and Ray. He was so frustrated. He didn't really know what to do. Maryann was trying as hard as she could to keep him—both the kids—from going over the edge. This broke Ray's heart—to see the shape the children were in, to know the marriage was really gone. He started drinking again and moved back in with us.

You said something about him going to Duffy's for the first time. Did he go back?

He did finally go back to Duffy's but didn't stay long. During the summer of '77 he'd gone off and started drinking again. Then he came to live with us again, but he'd learned at Duffy's how to taper himself off with reduced danger of seizures by having what he called "hummers."

Hummers? What are hummers?

Hummers are time-controlled shots of liquor. Ray had bottles of a kind of booze he hated to drink, the same kind they had given him at Duffy's. There was a time schedule. He'd start with a drink every half hour. Then, a day later, you taper off to a shot every hour; then, a day or two after that, one every two hours; then later every three hours, and so on.

What was Ray's hummer—the drink he hated most?

The cheapest possible bourbon. He gave the bottles to Amy and me, so he couldn't get at them, and he kept us on a schedule. Day after day, and night after night, we'd pour his hummers. I believe those days and nights were the lowest of the low he'd ever felt in his life. Sitting alone in our living room, sometimes in the dark—his marriage was gone—fearing he'd never write again, and that he had nothing. Whatever he owned—about one carload of books, manuscripts, a few personal items, some old clothing, a few artworks—had been packed in about six boxes and stored in the garage of the church next door.

All this happened even after the publication of Will You Please Be Quiet, Please? *Had he given up writing altogether?*

Yes. He thought this was as far as he would get. He said that more than once. One book and that was it. He knew he had to beat alcoholism first or his life was gone; he would die.

He'd been at our house a week, tapering off on his hummers and going to AA meetings at St. James Church. He looked out the window one morning and saw the church was having a bazaar. His few belongings had been spread out in the churchyard, ready to be sold. His manuscripts, his books, his few items of clothing, his artwork, whatever he had. So he and Amy and I had to go through the humiliation of going up to the ladies running the bazaar and saying, "No, this is not for sale. These are my belongings; there must be some mistake." Later we saw him sitting in our living room, all broken up, in grief, in tears. He has a poem in *Fires* called "Distress Sale" that captures those feelings.

Was this, then, the turning point?

He dried out in that apartment in San Francisco. This was after the second Duffy's at Myrtledale experience, which he could no longer afford. So he had to do it on his own. When he was off all the hummers and completely dried out, he only hung around San Francisco for a few weeks before he went to the Southern Methodist Writers' Conference in Dallas, where he met Tess Gallagher for the first time. Although they both maintained that they didn't meet

romantically there, seeds were sown for something to happen between them in the future.

What happened when he returned from the conference?

One of Ray's oldest friends, the writer Richard Day, helped him get
a house up in McKinleyville, near where Day was teaching at
Humboldt State, the college where Ray had received his B.A. He
knew he had to get out of San Francisco, away from the people,
places, and things that are discussed in the twelve-step program. I'm
not sure, but Ray might have had one more bad time with drinking,
just before he went up to McKinleyville and moved into this nice
house. But he finally managed to stay sober up there.

Did he start writing again there?

He tried. He had a room all set up for writing. He wasn't writing very
much, but he pulled off a great scam. He had written an outline for
a novel which was something like the German side of the story told
in *The African Queen,* and he had received an advance for the book
idea from McGraw-Hill. I'm not sure he had every intention of
writing the novel when he wrote the outline, but anybody could look
at this outline and look at Ray's stories and wonder how in the world
he was going to write that kind of book. He often joked, years later,
that he was still getting notes every so often from McGraw-Hill
asking how the novel was coming along. He'd tell them it was
coming just fine. So I believe he used this money to get by on in
McKinleyville; and there began a wonderful period of emerging from
alcoholism, learning how to survive and be happy with sobriety. It is
all very similar to the story "Chef's House." Maryann did go up and
live with him that fall. In many ways they were like kids again. They
went fishing every day, and played bingo, and visited old friends at
Humboldt State. This was the real beginning of his recovery. He
never had a drink again.

But they didn't live happy ever after, did they?

No, things fell apart because the children were in such terrible
difficulty. His daughter, Chris, and her boyfriend again ran into some

trouble with the law. All of Ray and Maryann's money had to go into bailing her out of her trouble. Chris came up to spend the holidays. Maryann worked as a waitress to make ends meet. Ray just couldn't be around all this—the family troubles, the guilt he felt that again they had no money. To keep himself sober, he had to get out and get away.

Where did he go from there?

He had a job to teach at the Goddard College program in Vermont— a two-week residency there—where he became good friends with Tobias Wolff and Richard Ford. Ray writes about this time in his essay "Friendship," and Tobias Wolff has remembered it vividly in his memoir about Ray. After that, I think Richard Ford set him up with a farmhouse somewhere in Illinois, but Ray couldn't stand the loneliness there, so he drove to Iowa City and moved into one of those tiny roadside cabins, a place called the Park Motel.

He had some money coming in from Goddard, and he also had some money he had borrowed from a student at Goddard. He was just barely getting by—really broke—living at the Park Motel, when Amy and I joined him. This time it was Amy and I landing on his doorstep. We had tried to make a life in New York City, me hoping to get a novel published and Amy trying to find work again in the theater. It was one of the snowiest and coldest winters on record in New York. We went belly up. And as down to the bone as Ray was, he told us we were welcome to join him in Iowa City, where we all had old friends and could get jobs, and we could rent the little cabin next to his. This brings us up to the spring of '78.

Did Ray start writing again in Iowa City?

He was beginning to try to work again. Ray was always working in one sense, inside his head. But at that point, I don't think he had written a new story in five years. He was living at the Park Motel, and he was struggling to get his voice back, to find his way to writing again. What I do know is that the story "Why Don't You Dance?" and a story called "Hooks," later called "Viewfinder," came across the desk of the *Iowa Review* at that time. They accepted "Why Don't You Dance?" So these two stories, as far as I know, were the first stories he had written since emerging from his terrible struggle with alcoholism. At that point he was convinced that he had stopped drinking, and he was ready to put his life together again.

You were with him at the time?

Yes, surely. We were the down-and-out in-laws this time. At first we didn't even have the ten dollars a night to rent out the cabin, and Ray lent it to us. It was all so much like typical early Carver country—tiny, seedy motel room, with a view out the back window of an even seedier-looking trailer park with strange goings-on day and night. Before that, just before we arrived, Maryann had come to Iowa City and they tried to patch things up for two or three weeks. Then a family emergency forced her to return back to Washington. Ray rented an apartment in Iowa City and Maryann moved back in again—one more try—and their son Vance also turned up that summer. Ray rented a second apartment to try to write in. Sometimes the whole family stayed in the houses where Amy and I had house-sitting jobs. It was a turbulent time. Ray called it "milling." We were milling around and getting nowhere. He was just emerging from his alcoholism, not quite a year sober yet. He left town for a while. Then Maryann left town, and him, and went back to California. Ray was pessimistic. One of his big concerns was if he'd be able to find a way to write again. He wasn't sure.

Was this about the time he landed the job in El Paso?

Yes, he had been offered a job teaching at the University of Texas at El Paso. That's where he went next. I had been in an auto accident that I couldn't pay for, so in addition to working a full day in the library I took on a night job washing dishes in a restaurant. Ray came to say goodbye to me in the alley behind the restaurant. It was a sad time. He gave me one of his big bear hugs and told me not to give up. Then I watched him drive off with those few boxes of his things all packed into an old beat-up Oldsmobile.

How would you describe his feelings at this time?

Well, he was down to bare minimum, but he was going off to a new job. And at least he was sober. He had hope now that something would happen to him, but he wasn't by any means optimistic.

But he did stay sober after that, didn't he?

He did stay sober. He never had another drink. Even when on the way to El Paso, about a hundred miles out or so, his car broke down. He called Tess, who was also teaching there, and that's how they got together. He traded that car for a bicycle. *[Laughs.]* He traded it right on the spot. That's the way it was with Ray. Disaster happened. But he now had a great story he would tell about how he had once actually traded his car for a bicycle.

How did you keep in touch after that?

We'd spend time with him on major holidays. And we'd see him for four or five days at least four times a year generally. His attitude then was that he was slowly coming out of it, and he was trying to get back into his writing. In fact, he was writing the darkest stories he ever wrote, the stories in *What We Talk About*. He had reached such a depth of depression and also a stylistic minimalism beyond which I think it was almost impossible to go—I mean in stories such as "A Serious Talk" and "One More Thing," the very dark stories about the breakup of a marriage which are so stark and full of pessimism about the world. It was as though he was writing stories about people for whom the worst has already happened. What's on the page is really just an echo of events in the past which have destroyed the people before the story even begins. The dark death of love, and hope, and faith, and youth.

Where was he when he was writing those stories?

He worked on those stories in El Paso, and in Syracuse when he got the job here. It was amazing to see the development in the work. He had discovered what I call a kind of *via meditiva* of writing fiction. The style of the writing itself is a kind of argument from absence. He concentrated, in details and in describing events, on what is *not* there, or on what has *not* happened. It's as though the stories prove, in a way, that love and hope and charity and the finer human emotions must still exist, if only because of their striking absence for his characters after what they have lived through. It's just incredibly fine writing.

Could you expand on that—give us some examples?

Sure. You'll notice that most of his stories of this period begin with an assertion in the first few lines. Then that is immediately followed by a contradiction. Note how Christmas is described by what is missing or wrong or absent in the Christmas description in "A Serious Talk," or the fact that the main assertion in the story is that a serious talk must happen between the main character and his wife—but of course the serious talk never happens. What I'm saying, I guess, is that Ray achieved a particular and extremely economical style by writing about what does not happen, by picking out what is missing, or by letting the reader know what should have happened for his characters but didn't. Even in certain choices of details, you can see this. One example I like can be found in the story "Feathers." In the description of the house in the country, almost the only detail about it is the chimney. Then a point is made that there was no smoke coming out of it. Just choosing that one detail of absence somehow enables the reader to see everything that surrounds that one thing that is missing. Or take "Cathedral." The important detail about the visitor is the absence of his ability to see. That absence becomes spiritually the very gift of sight for the narrator. Do you see what I mean, or am I way off base? To my mind, anyway, this *via negativa* seems to be at the core of Ray Carver's writing.

Was that much a departure from his earlier stories?

One thing I know about Ray from reading his manuscripts and talking to him about his life was that some of his stories in *Will You Please Be Quiet, Please?* were around in some form or another from the time he was eighteen. His basic writing style didn't change all that much, really. But in *What We Talk About When We Talk About Love* and some of the stories in *Cathedral* his writing took a very deliberate turn to an even more negative minimalist story. His style reached a stripped-down extreme beyond which I don't think he could or even wanted to go. He said in an interview once that he had to step back from that extreme style because he couldn't go farther. Later you can see how in some of the stories in *Cathedral* and the seven new stories in *Where I'm Calling From,* the fiction and the writing becomes more ample—broader—and actually allows love and hope and compassion to come in, to be a part of the story, to be there.

Ray wrote often about the importance of revision—how rewarding it was, how he actually liked to revise—

Ray had a fascinating attitude about his stories. I consider it a liberating attitude for young writers. Sometimes he'd simply change a few elements of a story, or he'd add a frame to the story, maybe change character names. He'd send out the version he thought best. Years later he might send out the other version. Two similar stories with different titles might appear in different published collections. Ray had no qualms about this. After all, they were like different stories to him. And he didn't hesitate to reapproach his stories even after they were published and rework them. The best example I can think of is "The Bath" and "A Small, Good Thing." He viewed his work as a continuing process and was constantly revising not only manuscripts, but even published stories.

For instance, "Distance" and "Everything Stuck to Him": "Distance" has a frame. It's a story that looks back from a balcony in Italy where the daughter has come to visit, and her father tells her the story of what he and his young wife went through one night when she was a baby, which is the same story as "Everything Stuck to Him." Ray had no trouble thinking of these as different stories and publishing them that way.

Ray's story "Intimacy," the story of a writer's visit to his ex-wife—as far as you know, did Ray make that visit?

I'm not sure that visit actually happened. But from personal experience, knowing both Ray and Maryann, I'm sure everything in that story had been said to Ray at one time or another. Ray and Maryann spoke often on the phone and wrote many letters back and forth. I know there is a tremendous sadness in Maryann now, and there has been for some time, about how the world—the literary media in particular—considers their relationship. She read all the reviews describing these down-and-out people in Ray's work, treating them like ragged low-lifes, most of them, saying how heartbreaking they are. Maryann is a proud, capable woman. She's an educated person, has a master's degree, and can quote from Jung and Blake and the major poets. She knows how hard she and Ray had it in the early days. She was his first sounding board. She helped edit all those early stories. She worked for nineteen years to keep Ray and the family together. Then to see their lives and his work so refracted and distorted to the world by critics, reviewers, and now even biographers, to see the most intimate portions of their lives shown in Ray's work treated that way—all of that really hurt her pride. And that's what "Intimacy" is about. It's the writer asking forgiveness for having allowed their lives to be so used and abused in his stories and by the world,—then, of course, the ironic twist of making use of that very apology as fresh meat for another story.

Are you saying this was Ray's way of seeking forgiveness, making amends? Or the route he took for another story?

No; life with Maryann was over, however much they still loved and cared for one another until his death. Ray was in love with Tess and was completely with her in his new life. He'd speak of the old life and the new life. The old life had a great many good things in it, but it ended with all the drinking and the "bad old days" and he'd never want to go back to that. I don't think he felt the need to ask forgiveness of anyone, not even Maryann. The new life was a life of acceptance; and all through this new life, he and Maryann were never enemies—never, no matter what happened. It's strange. She and Tess are so much alike. There are many differences, of course. But they're both, at heart, small-town Washington girls from working-class families. They're both literate, sensitive, self-made and self-educated women, and both are incredibly strong and willful. Maybe I'm wrong, but I see them as similar in so many ways that Ray's deep love for one and then the other becomes totally comprehensible.

How did he react with you in his new life?

We were friends. We were family. We talked on the phone at least twice a month and visited each other often. I remember when *What We Talk About When We Talk About Love* was reviewed on the front page of the *New York Times Book Review*, Ray called up and said, "Did you see that? Would you believe it? Who would have thought it five years ago?" He was like a child at Christmas with every good review or piece of good news. He'd want to come over and play—share his gift, his success. He was astounded at the new reception of his stories. After so many years of rejection—the financial struggles, the drinking, even giving up writing—now, when he least expected it, the world embraced him. He never ceased to be amazed at that. What was happening, I believe, is that our culture finally caught up to Ray's style and subjects. The disillusionment of the seventies and eighties now suddenly found itself reflected in his work. Of course, he had been writing some of these stories since the sixties—or at least his basic style had been there all along. He was ahead of his time.

Was he able to enjoy this turnaround?

He was fascinated by it and by the smallest kinds of pleasures it enabled him to enjoy. He'd check into a nice hotel room in New York. He'd laugh and quote his version of the Pinter line, "A person feels like he has a chance in a room like this." Just going out to dinner was a big occasion. And he'd always want to share this feeling with his friends. He was generous with his success. He helped so many other writers, his friends and his students. And in a literary way he was still growing. That was the most miraculous thing of all to him. Those years between Syracuse and Port Angeles were very productive.

How did Tess contribute to this new life?

Tess was instrumental in getting his life organized. From all the chaos of the past, Tess was able to step in and establish order, manage things so Ray wouldn't have to worry about bill collectors or other distractions—how to make ends meet, or how to find writing time. Tess would unplug the phone and put up a sign that said No Visitors. Ray often said how happy they were. They were having fun together, too. Ray wrote the vast body of his work during this new life.

Ray wrote a great deal of poetry as well as fiction. How did he view his poetry?

I think writing poetry, more than fiction, was his first love. I don't believe that, after Ray was turned down for financial aid as a young poet that year at Iowa, that he ever gave up his youthful dream of being accepted by the world as a poet. Poetry, more than fiction, was an obsession for him. If he had a choice between writing a story or a poem—if writers really have that kind of choice—I think he'd favor the poem.

Is that why he wrote only poetry after he learned about his illness?

I couldn't say. But after he finished the manuscript for *Where I'm Calling From,* he and I had a talk about fiction and poetry. He wanted more than anything to complete another book of poems and was happy to be back to poetry. He was, I think, very noncalculating when it came to the impulses for his work. He wrote what he felt like writing. He followed his instincts and his own gut feelings about what to work on. I don't believe he ever violated that. When he completed the manuscript for *Where I'm Calling From,* he was also a little concerned. In this talk we had, he was feeling written out with his fiction. So he was naturally looking forward to getting back to his poems.

Was that before or after he knew he was ill?

This conversation definitely took place before he knew he was ill. I should explain; a lot of people kept urging him to write less poetry and more fiction. We were talking about that, and he told me that he wasn't sure if he had another story in him, that he had to fill his well again. I believe, for Ray, that always meant going back to writing poetry.

By that time he'd written "Errand," a distinct departure from his previous stories. Do you believe that was the direction his stories would have followed if he had continued in fiction?

He had a lot of fun with "Errand." I was at Yaddo when that story came out, and it so happened there was a copy of Henri Troyat's biography of Chekhov around. James Salter noticed that the death scene in the biography and a large part of the death scene in "Errand" was almost exactly alike, almost word for word. That caused quite a stir and discussion among the writers there.

Ray and I talked on the phone a day or two later. He told me that he had read the biography, was fascinated by it, and decided to use it when he got the idea for his story. To his mind it was no different than using parts of a story one of his friends had told him around the table. But it really is interesting that he used the primary text out of the biography and then turned it so completely into a Ray Carver story. He laughed at how someone had actually caught him at it, then said he might just do that same kind of story with the biographies of other writers he admired, like de Maupassant, Dostoevsky, and Kafka.

So you saw a new departure in his later work?

The stories that broke him into something entirely new were "Blackbird Pie" and "Errand." I think "Blackbird Pie" is almost Nabokovian in its use of cryptic messages from the wife—a story at least partly about the interpretation of language. Ray was definitely playing with something different here. And "Errand," as I said, plays with the idea of writing a story based on the biography of another writer and making that story his own. I believe he might have been thinking of going off in those directions if he had lived long enough.

Which of his earlier stories were your favorites?

From the early work I'd choose "Neighbors" and "Are These Actual Miles?" Those two stories reflect to me the desperation of that time, and they are so beautifully crafted. "Neighbors" is a classic, a doppelganger story full of black humor that is characteristically Ray's.

Which of his later stories?

I'd have to say "Where I'm Calling From." It's certainly his most honest story. Ray was always honest in his fiction—that is to say that he was true to his personal vision of what is real and important in life. But that story goes a step beyond. Ray was revealing the depth of his own fear, his intense self-doubts, the ragged edge of his own recovery, and how precarious and tenuous recovery really was. To his mind, recovery from alcoholism may have indeed depended on luck alone. Ray was a great believer that he suddenly got lucky.

Lucky?

Yes, he considered himself fortunate. Even when he was so sick, he reminded himself and everyone else just what he had come back from. When he was going into surgery for lung cancer here at St. Joseph's Hospital, he was joking with us. He said there was the old life, and then there had been the new life. There he was lying on the gurney, a blue shower cap on his head, prepped for surgery. "Well, I'm on to the next new life," he said, as they wheeled him out of the room.

Then in the spring, when they gave him his honorary doctorate in Hartford, he was so happy. He turned to everyone and said, "Well, it's Dr. Carver now. You'll all have to start calling me doctor," he said and laughed. It was just two months before he died. That was really the top for him, even though he was suffering so badly from cancer and had the brain tumor and all the radiation therapy. From Hartford, he went on to give a reading at the Endicott Bookstore and sign copies of *Where I'm Calling From.* People were spilling out into the street. He was exhausted from the illness and could barely read. It was a short reading. Then he signed books for hours. The next day, he was inducted into the American Academy and Institute of Arts and Letters. He was so proud of that, to stand up there and be honored by his peers and admired by the public. It was a miracle to him. Then he went out to the reception and celebrated with so many old friends. The next day there was another book signing at the Scribner's bookstore. I've never seen anything like it. About twenty writers were there signing books, but there were as many people lined up at Ray's table, waiting for a handshake and signature, as you might see in line for a first-run movie—hundreds of people. He kept turning to me and saying, "Can you believe this? Isn't this just amazing? Who would have thought this?" That was his attitude. He was so proud of all the attention, and he was so good with all those people. Finally, they had to shut the bookstore down. We were out in the street later and there were still people waiting.

How was he able to get through all that?

Well, you see, he had managed to convince both the press and his editors that he had beaten his cancer. Up until mid-June, maybe he had convinced himself, as well as the world, that he had beaten it. When he was asked how he was doing, he'd say, "I'm getting stronger every day."

He touched people at such a personal level . . .

It really is amazing and wonderful. I've taught Ray Carver in two languages, in the original here and in Spanish in Latin America. So many people all over the world are still just discovering his work. In Buenos Aires there's a bookshop that also serves coffee and sandwiches. They serve a salad called "Carver" and a sandwich called "Cathedral." Ray's on a restaurant menu in Argentina! The Cathedral Sandwich is cheese and lettuce on white bread—the simplest things. Everybody, it seems, is reading him down there, even though the book in paperback costs the equivalent of twenty dollars for people earning one or two hundred dollars a month. They're buying it and xeroxing it and passing it around. And I know this is happening all over the world.

It's so sad to think there will never be another Carver story.

I'm not so sure of that. There's a play, *Carnations*, that I don't think has been published. There are film treatments he wrote or collaborated on. There must be other writing. Somewhere in this world there's sure to be a box with forgotten manuscripts in it. I'll just bet that one day, we'll be seeing stories and poems we've never read before. And there's always the great work he left us. For me, still, every time I read a story or poem by Ray, it's a new experience.

You're not alone there.

August 18, 1990
Syracuse, New York

MARYANN CARVER

Yet we'd both long before given up our personal selves
for his literature. I had to lose my life to gain my life,
so to speak. Looked at another way, Lenny Michaels
was right. We did pay for those stories with our lives.
Ray is dead, and I've lost my identity.

And about that story, "Intimacy," God bless
Ray. He wrote whatever came to him and if he could
use anything, he did.

Maryann Carver rejected my request for a meeting. She would not discuss those personal matters over which she had maintained a steadfast silence all these years. I told her of my talk with her sister Amy when I interviewed Doug Unger, and how Bill Kittredge and Lenny Michaels had recalled her with such affectionate concern. She said she would meditate on it.

I meet with Maryann in the restored 1910 farmhouse she moved from its original site to the tract of land her grandfather had homesteaded. We are seven miles from Blaine, a border town in the northwest corner of Washington. She has converted the old house into Mariposa, home of the blue butterfly—a spiritual retreat and learning center for those seeking guidance, comfort, and transformation. I see a table covered with copies of Ray's books, snapshots, memorabilia, and scented candles. Near it is a piano with a photograph of Ray in place of the sheet music.

Maryann is introspective as she considers each question. She is exploring a lifetime of unexpressed remembrance, and she will tell it her way. We break twice so she may supervise a group practicing Reiki in the basement. Reiki, she tells me, is a Japanese word symbolizing the relationship between Universal Life Energy and our personal life force, and would I care to participate in a session? We go down to the basement, a shadowy, candle-lit room, where a dozen people seem to be meditating as they walk in slow random patterns around the room. I smell incense and hear muted Japanese music. Maryann leads me to a padded table.

I lie down and soon feel a pair of clasped hands gently elevate and support my head like a pillow. Other hands massage my feet and toes, while fingertips drum swiftly, but softly, up, down, and across my body. I close my eyes. I meditate on how I could have journeyed no further in the continental U.S.A. from my house in South Miami, than to this house, this table, this trip.

Sam Halpert: Can you recall the first time you saw Ray?

Maryann Carver: Oh, yes. It was in June, 1955. I was almost fifteen and he had just turned seventeen. I was working at my first real job at a place called the Spudnut Shop. It was a doughnut shop in Union Gap, Washington, a suburb of Yakima. Ray's mother was also employed there, so I knew his mother before I knew him; but I didn't know he was Ella's son. So this very good-looking young man came in with his younger brother and sat down on a stool. When I first saw him I had this incredible intuition that he was going to be the father of my children. Of course I didn't know in those days about past lives and that sort of thing. I just had that immediate recognition when I saw him. We looked at each other and smiled with delight. We knew each other.

When did you and Ray marry?

It was on June 7, 1957. We went together for two years before we were married, and for most of that time I was attending a private college preparatory school for girls.

Did Ray show any desire to be a writer at that time?

Well, Ray always wanted to write. He wanted to be a writer from the third grade on.

Where did you live after you were married?

During our first year, we lived in Ray's family doctor's apartment that was underneath his office. We'd clean his office in payment for rent and utilities, and he even paid for the newspaper and telephone. That was our daily job.

Did you decide that Ray should go on to college?

We had talked about that for as long as we had known each other. As I said, I had gone to a private school, comparable to a junior college. When a girl graduated from there she could go to Vassar or Wellesley or wherever. I had a scholarship from the University of Washington to study law. Ray and I had discussed all this. We wrote to each other every day while I was at school; and when I wasn't at school, we saw each other every day. Then, when he moved with his family to California, we kept up this incredible correspondence. I remember writing to him that I was working ten and twelve hours a day so that I could get a scholarship and that I wouldn't be happy with anyone who didn't want to go to college.

Did Ray share your feelings about college?

No, Ray didn't want to go to college. He wanted to work and make money to buy a car, and a phonograph, and clothes and things like that. And that's exactly what he did for a year.

Were you married at the time?

No, he graduated a year ahead of me.

What was Ray doing during that year?

He worked part of the year down in California and earned the money to buy a car, the hi-fi, and some of the material things that he really lusted for. And that was more important for him, at that time, than to go to college. Then he missed me, and I missed him, so he came back to Washington. I was at the girls' school, so he stayed with his aunt in Yakima. He'd come down to see me at school in Walla Walla as often as the school permitted me to have a guest. Then, later that year, he and two friends decided that they were going to South America. He had been heavily influenced by the movie *King Solomon's Mines,* having seen it about fourteen times. He loved movies—we both did. Anyway, he wanted to pick diamonds out of the mouth of the Amazon River. It was absolutely catastrophic to me. We would be separated. He planned to be gone for two years on this great adventure, but we planned for it emotionally and every other way. We had a very melancholic Christmas in 1956 waiting for him to make this trip.

Did he actually go on this expedition?

Yes, he left in January. He and his friends got down to Mexico as far as Guaymas.

How were they traveling?

One of them had a beat-up old car.

They were going to drive down to the Amazon?

[Laughter.] Oh, yes. Ray knew he wanted to be a writer. He wanted to travel, to see the world, have adventure. At the same time he wanted me, and he tried to juggle these things forevermore, really. All the early things were definitely there. I unearthed some letters from high school days just last week and it's amazing how all the Carver themes were in these letters written when he was seventeen years old.

How did the expedition work out?

Well, the boys had a falling out. One of them turned out to be an alcoholic, even at that age, and cantankerous. The two other boys were closer to each other than to Ray. There was some kind of fight. It had to do with *[laughs]* a crawdad or some horrible creature they had caught in the water down there and brought back to camp. As I recall, Ray caught this thing and was proud of it, and the drunk ridiculed it; and to make a long story short, they had a fight over it. And so in a matter of three weeks after he left, Ray arrived back in Redding, California, which was close enough to his parents so they could come and get him. He was absolutely broke and hadn't had a thing to eat for about three days. His dad laughed about how Ray ate two breakfasts when he got him. That was the end of that adventure, and of course I was very glad that he was back. He came up to Yakima and worked there that spring until I graduated in June. He came to the formal dances at the school and brought his friends down. His friends went with my friends and we had a lovely spring.

What was the name of that school?

St. Paul's School for Girls, an Episcopalian school in Walla Walla.

Then you married shortly after you graduated?

Four days after I graduated. Ray planned the whole wedding with my family. He bought the rings and worked hard on it. He had just turned nineteen, but he was kind of ageless. He could go hunting or fishing with his father's friends who were well up into their forties or older, and he'd be treated as if he were one of them.

Did you and Ray have any plans?

Well, all the time I was at the girls' school, I was very idealistic and studious. I saw my role in life to be a scholar. I knew I wouldn't be happy unless we got a very good higher education. Nobody in Ray's family had ever gone to college, so there was no tradition for it. He hoped he could just read a lot, which he always did, and that would prepare him adequately to be a writer. He had an extraordinary vocabulary—just like my mother. I could ask Ray the meaning of any word, and he'd know exactly what it meant and how to spell it; but he didn't particularly like school. He wasn't a natural student the way I was. However, the biggest plan in our lives was for Ray to become a first-rate, world-class writer.

But eventually he did go to college?

Yes, but because it was in the late fifties, and he was the male and I was the female, it was the logical thing along sexist lines in those days that he would be the one to go. I went along with that, because I knew I would eventually go too, because I was so motivated. But it was important that he get started in school as soon as possible, and he did.

What school did he go to?

He started in the fall of '57 at Yakima Community College and attended for a year before we moved to California.

What prompted the move to California?

My mother and younger sister had gone down to California on a trip, and my sister was gung-ho to move there. She had some friends there, and she was a great beauty and brain and full of life and wanted to be where the action was—which she thought was in California, not in Washington. My mother, who was a teacher, got a job down there in the Bay Area, but she also bought a house that appealed to her in Paradise, California, near Chico. She thought that Ray and I and the baby could move down and live in that house, because she didn't want to leave me behind in Washington. She also persuaded us to move down because there was a four-year college in Chico that Ray could go to.

What about your education?

As far as my going to college, although I was the one with the high grades and the law school scholarship, when I mentioned going to junior college in Yakima and wanted to go desperately—my sister offered to take care of our baby girl, who had been born in December—Ray said, "What are you going to do with the baby— put her in a suitcase?" That so inhibited me that I hung back and didn't go and decided to become a good mother and all that.

Was Ray eager for college then?

Well, I had pointed out to him all along that as a writer he would benefit from a good education. He needed to read good writers, to know about them, and history, and art—

How long was he at Chico?

He went there from 1958 to 1960. I might say at this point that, when I went to private school, I had to read twenty books over the summer, and when I had these lists of books, and Ray would accompany me to the library where I'd check out Tolstoy, Flaubert, and Chekhov, for example—well, Ray had never heard of these writers before. I read all these books and told him what they were about, showed him their styles, and so forth. He'd look at them and realize there was more to read than Thomas Costain and Edgar Rice Burroughs.

What happened after the two years at Chico?

We moved over to Humboldt where he went to the state university, and after a year I started there, too. Actually, I don't think this is too well known, but for the first thirteen years of our marriage, one or the other or both of us were in college, without any money, pursuing an education. Thirteen years . . .

Why do you suppose he didn't write about the academic life in his stories?

It wasn't his primary interest in life, though he did enjoy the many friends we had from school, and he enjoyed studying drama, history, and some of the literature he encountered in good classes. However, Ray was always rather eccentric—always his own person. He never, in those days, jumped through hoops to please anyone or to placate the system. For example, one time he signed up for one more course than he wanted to take, merely to have enough units on paper to qualify for a federal loan. He never attended the class and took an *F* in it, which brought his point grade down, but none of this bothered him; whereas, if I took a course, I'd have to get an *A* in it.

Can you tell us the name of the first story he wrote and when he completed it?

All the time I was at St. Paul's, long before he met John Gardner or anyone else, Ray was taking a course from the Palmer Institute of Writing, which his father working at the mill paid for and was proud his son was taking.

Was this a home-study course?

Yes, and Ray would religiously do those assignments. He'd feel very guilty if he didn't. Later on and always, if he weren't writing for any reason, he'd feel guilty just like in high school. He used to send me assignments all the time when I was at St. Paul's. Maybe it was a character sketch, like a heavy woman baking bread, and you could smell the bread. Or else maybe it was to describe a scene—

Aside from these correspondence school assignments, which would you call Ray's first story?

Well, he had written some science-fiction stories before we moved to Chico, but when he got into John Gardner's writing class down there, he stopped being interested in writing about little green monsters and the like. He began the He/She stories in a contemporary literary mode.

Can you recall a story he wrote at Chico?

Yes, he wrote "Furious Seasons," and it created a tremendous stir among his classmates and the faculty at Chico.

Was this the story he later included in his collection of the same name? When did he write it?

Yes. This was in 1959, because I remember the green house we lived in and how old the babies were then.

Was this while he was in John Gardner's class?

Yes.

What did Gardner think of the story?

Oh, I know he thought it was outrageously good and taught the hell out of it in Ray's class—I went to listen. He also included the story in the college literary magazine he and another faculty member, Lennis Dunlap, were editing at the time. But Gardner was very cool and sophisticated. He wasn't one to lose control of a relationship or be too carried away about any one student's work. His students were always challenged to outdo their last effort. But it was very obvious—reading between the lines, so to speak—that both Gardner and Dunlap knew they were encountering someone very special in Ray.

Which was the first story actually accepted by a publisher?

Ray's first story accepted was "Pastoral" by *Western Humanities Review*. He received two copies for payment. This was in 1962, when we were living in Humboldt. As a matter of fact, I still have the letter of acceptance. On the very same day, *Target,* a magazine in Arizona, accepted Ray's poem "Brass Ring," his first poetry acceptance.

We were on top of the world. It seemed that if you did the

right things, the right things would happen. It was incredibly encouraging. We were ecstatic and partied for three days. We interrupted our friends' dinner—the poets David and Charlene Palmer—to celebrate our great news, our great joy. They dropped everything and we called other friends, who called other friends. We called Dick and Bonnie Day and brought them into the celebration. The Days, Palmers, and Carvers were wonderful friends despite the fact that they were ten years older than we. They taught us, they helped us, and they loved us. Dick Day was Ray's writing professor at the time, and Dave Palmer was a master librarian at Humboldt and a published poet. His wife, Charlene, was a poet and a very fine painter as well. They were all dear, dear friends who rejoiced in every success Ray or we had.

Why had you moved to Humboldt from Chico?

Because there was work for Ray in the lumber industry. There was nothing in Chico except working in the college library for a dollar an hour.

How did things work out in Humboldt?

Ray graduated from Humboldt in 1963. The first year we were there I worked for the phone company, where I felt left out of school life and lonely in general. I had transferred over to Humboldt from the Chico office, and altogether I had been working at the phone company since I was eighteen. I'd started when my second baby, my son Vance, was eight months old. I'd get a paycheck every two weeks and within half an hour the money would be gone. By the time I paid the babysitter and all the bills, there was nothing left; and then I'd work another two weeks, being dead broke all the time. I didn't enjoy the work, though out of pride I excelled at it, and I didn't relate to the crass type of people I worked with. That was a bad year for me. I worked days, and Ray went to school days and worked in a mill at night, so it was a grim year for him, too, except for a good writing class he was taking and for some friends he met at school.

Then one morning at ten o'clock when I was on coffee break—I was twenty-one years old—something snapped in me, and I left the building in a hurry, saying I was ill, and took myself over to

Humboldt. By five o'clock I had been admitted to school—I had the registrar call long distance to St. Paul's for my SAT scores. He got me a loan for tuition and lined me up for subsequent scholarships, which I received every semester for two years. When Ray came home that night and I told him I was going to go to school, too—that I'd found a house near the college, a nursery school for the kids nearby, and a part-time job, all in one day—he was just blown away. *[Laughs.]*

That's marvelous. How did it turn out?

From then on in, things were really pretty good for us there. Ray quit the mill and worked at the college library, and together we had lots of friends. For the next two years we both went to school. Ray graduated in mid-year '63 and went down to Berkeley and got a job at the University of California in the biology library. I finished school in June and moved to Berkeley with the children. In the meantime, Professor Dick Day was working to get Ray a grant at the University of Iowa at the Writers Workshop. And that summer, the grant came through. Ray got a thousand dollars, and by August '63 we were off to Iowa City. We piled everything into our '53 Chevy— "Old Faithful," we called it—with a rack on the top that carried all our belongings, and the four of us were on our way.

What was it like for you when you arrived in Iowa?

Well, first we stayed at a trailer park, but then our application for student housing was approved. I had been great through all the moves and transitions that we had gone through up until then, but I did just sit down on the bed and cry when I saw the Quonset hut, a World War II relic that served as University of Iowa married student housing. There were cement floors; open cupboards in the kitchen; the hot water tank was in the middle of the living room floor. The children's room was like a cell with two little bunks and a tiny window. It was quite depressing. The weather was cold and I just sat there crying for a while. Actually, I turned that place into one of the most charming homes we ever had. I was really challenged by it. I had to get down and paint the cement floors and go out to buy a carpet from the Salvation Army, make curtains for the open cupboards, and turn the place into something we could tolerate. And, as always, we had hard times through those early years as students, whether we were in Berkeley, or Iowa, or Humboldt, or wherever.

You were living the Carver story.

Oh, but we also had a tremendous amount of fun. We were popular people, we had lots of friends, and we entertained a lot. We were young, and we loved good times. And when we didn't have friends over, Ray and I had our own party every single night of our lives. At the end of the day, when we completed our jobs and work at school and finished with the children, we'd get together for a cup of coffee, talk over the day, and laugh. Ray was a very funny man, and we were funny together. Year in and year out we were crazy in love with each other.

We had our first turkey that we prepared ourselves in Iowa. We not only put on a holiday dinner for our children, but for half the workshop as well. I worked at the University Athletic Club—a country club—as a waitress to bring in the bulk of our living. I put the turkey in the oven, then I rushed off to work, and Ray watched the dinner and the children. When I got off work, we had a feast, a party, with our kids and our friends.

How did things break for you after that?

After that, my father died in January, and I had to go back to the West Coast with the children for a month. Losing my dad was a devastating blow to me. When I got back to Iowa, I had to go right back to work and try to get caught up financially. I felt sad and very pressured. That spring, Ray went through a bout of depression himself, which he frequently did because of our financial struggle. We'd studied existentialism, and *angst* and melancholy went with the trade in those days, and Ray was good at it. However, he told me long after we were married that from an early age, before I had ever met him, as a teenager he'd considered suicide several times.

Had Ray started his heavy drinking by then?

No, he would drink at a time of crisis or something, and we would drink socially on some weekends, but alcohol definitely wasn't a major problem then.

How was his writing going at the time?

Ray wrote well in Iowa—for example, "Sixty Acres," "The Student's Wife," "Will You Please Be Quiet, Please?" That spring, after we had had such a desperate time financially and all that, I checked around and found out that Ray had more publications than anybody else in the workshop. But he was very quiet and very shy and sat in the back of the room and didn't impose himself on anybody, and the powers that be simply didn't know he was there. They'd champion other writers who weren't anywhere near as good as Ray. I don't want to name names, but the fact of the matter is nobody has ever heard of them again, with the exception of Joy Williams. That's exactly what I went down and told Paul Engle when I found out they were deciding on grants for the following year. They were reading manuscripts for the grants that weekend, and Ray hadn't been invited to participate. I was a bit of a firebrand in those days, especially when it came to my family. I was going to make sure we survived. I was so angry. Ray had worked so hard at his writing and was so good—head and shoulders above everyone else—yet nobody knew he was even there. He received no attention whatsoever, and we were starving, practically.

What did you do?

Well, one morning I got my hair done *[laughs]*, and put on my best dress. I didn't tell Ray, but I gathered all his published stories and his manuscript in progress, which was *Will You Please Be Quiet, Please?*, and I went down to the Writers' Workshop. I went down at 8:00 A.M. to Paul Engle's office and asked to see him. He wasn't there, and I said, "That's fine, I'll wait." I waited all day. The secretary started looking at me, and so did all the writers and the faculty, one by one, as they came in and heard the story. *[Laughs.]* Ray loved this story. A few years ago they asked him to attend an event at the University of Iowa honoring Paul Engle, and Ray wrote me how well he remembered this incident and how pleased he was I'd done what I had. Anyway, I just sat there all day with Ray's stuff and nothing to eat, and finally around four in the afternoon Paul Engle showed up. He asked me into his office, but he picked up his mail at the same time. He asked me what was on my mind, but when I started to tell him he kept reading his mail. So I stopped talking, and after two minutes he noticed that, but I told him it was okay: "Why don't you just finish reading your mail?" He realized, of course, that he'd been rude and pushed the mail aside and began listening to me. I asked him if he remembered what happened when Tennessee Williams came to Iowa. Everybody there knew how Williams had written *The Glass Menagerie* and the teachers there had rejected it, not given him his degree, and had virtually ridden him out of town on a rail. Engle perked up his ears. He was half-insulted and half-interested. I told him he had another situation almost exactly like that with my husband. "Nobody knows he's here, nobody knows he exists, and nobody even reads his manuscripts." I told him Ray had more published stories and poems than any other student there, and he was a far better writer than many of the faculty members. I showed Engle all the publications and the work in progress, and he agreed to give it to a faculty member to read over the weekend. The upshot of it was that John Clellan Holmes went wild over it after reading the manuscripts. He came back on Monday raving about Ray's work and passed it around to other powers that were.

How did Ray react to all this?

Talk about Ray's drinking—well, when Ray came back to the house *[laughs]* he noticed his manuscripts were gone. Tampering with Ray's work was just anathema. It was his baby. I wasn't to touch works in progress; the kids weren't to touch them. His career, his writing—he and I put it on such a pedestal. We'd sacrifice anything for that, first, last, and always. Anyway, he noticed his things were gone, and when I fessed up what I had done, he stayed drunk all weekend. *[Laughs.]* He was actually pleased.

What was the result of your effort?

After the faculty read the stories, they offered him a stipend for the following year.

That must have been gratifying. Did it make life easier?

No, we went back to California in June.

Why?

As I said, my father had died. My father was the first hero in my life, and Ray was my next. My father's death was hard on me, and I was homesick for the coast. However, *I* didn't want to leave, because I wanted Ray to get his master's from Iowa; but Ray himself wanted to go back.

He wanted to quit?

Yes, Ray felt he wanted to move on at the time. The grass must be greener elsewhere and so on. Other people were packing up because it was time to go, and Ray got itchy feet, too. Ray even quit the English department at Berkeley when he was teaching there. He had a job teaching creative writing and he turned down a second year. We heard he was only the second person in history to quit the English department at Berkeley.

When did he have that job at Berkeley?

It must have been 1972–73, when Lenny Michaels recommended him for the job. I'm just making the point that Ray always did what he wanted to do. If he wanted to leave Iowa before he got his degree there, and his emotional urge was such that he wanted to do it, he would do it. He was never compromised by awards or thoughts of future gain. He wasn't on any treadmill. He thought for himself.

After Iowa, did you go back to Washington or California?

California. When we came back, we went to Sacramento, where Ray's parents lived. We had a hard time then. Ray had a hard time finding work. He had his B.A. from Humboldt, and a year at Iowa. He had been in school since 1957 and it was now 1964, but nobody was impressed with his credentials. He tried all kinds of little jobs. One job was as desk clerk in a hotel. *[Laughs.]* Before he put in one shift, he had me deliver a letter to them telling he wouldn't be coming. He worked as a stock boy at Weinstock's Department

Store. There's this father of two children, a writer with all these publications, and his degree, and he's working as a stock boy. The final blow came when he was fired for stealing cookies, and of course he hadn't taken their cookies. Somebody else had, but they fired the whole crew. These were hard times for Ray. I was working. I always worked. I always had to.

Did Ray keep up with his writing?

Yes, he never stopped writing. That was always his main focus, along with me and the family. He had a job as janitor at Mercy Hospital in Sacramento, and he was glad to get it. He held that job for two and a half years. First on the day shift, where he really had to work, mopping, housekeeping, and doing hospital beds. Then he got on the night shift, which was a gravy train, and he had his days free to write.

Do you remember which stories he wrote during this time?

I guess I could just go down the table of contents of the collection *Will You Please Be Quiet, Please?* I edited every one of those stories before anybody did. Ray would encourage me to do what John Gardner did: take a pencil and strike out any words I thought didn't belong. I was perfectly free to edit a story or poem in any way. And without fail he would take fifty percent of my suggestions and ignore the other fifty percent. We'd sit down with a story, and I'd explain my corrections, and he'd agree or not. But it was always a joint effort to come out with the best.

Did you recognize yourself in these stories?

Oh, I saw myself in these stories, of course; but Ray was a fiction writer, and he took liberties, God knows.

And he put you in his poetry as well—

Oh, always, right down to "Notes Found In A Bathrobe," written at the end when he was so ill. I—you know, I can modestly say that I was his lifelong muse, from the time we were first together. As a matter of fact, I was the first lady he ever had. *[Pause.]*

He was always six years behind writing about a reality that occurred. I was amazed, for instance, at how he could remember conversations he heard at a party and write about it six years later. It was consistent—six years, right down the line. It took him six years to process the material.

Did you see that pattern later on?

I'd wonder at what was going to happen after we had been apart and divorced—to see where his writing would take off then. And almost six years after we were divorced, he died, at the end of the . . . *[Pause.]*

How did you two keep in touch after the divorce?

Oh, we always wrote letters and called up—nearly every week. We had like an underground friendship—more than a friendship. He resented the word *friendship*. As he said in a poem, we separated and became friends. The ironies are quite clear. He was tuning in to the source. And I'd write a letter with a teasing little anecdote to feed him some material when he needed it—including his last summer, when I wrote him a long letter that organized our life together from my point of view, hoping that it would give him incentive and motivation beyond what he already had to live and put this material in a novel. I thought it over carefully and then gave him my material that I was using in my own book.

How did he reply to that?

He wrote back a long letter saying, now, that's the kind of letter he liked to get, with a beginning, a middle, and end—you know, a real story. He was *pleased!*

Around what date was this?

About the end of May '88. I was praying for his life and gathering cancer information from all over the world. I had been to a lecture in Vancouver given by a man from Berkeley who knew all about free radicals, germanium, and all the most avant-garde effective things that could be done. And Ray was interested in this, too, and began to pursue my information; but it was too late. I didn't realize that until I got the call. *[Pause. She goes into the kitchen and talks to her granddaughter for a few minutes.]*

Could you tell us something about Ray's work habits?

Whenever he could afford it, Ray would rent a room where he could be alone to do his writing. Even in 1961, when we had a big house in Arcata, which was the first time he rented space away from home, he rented a room elsewhere to write in. He had one later in Sacramento; he had one later in Palo Alto, and in Cupertino. We sacrificed necessities, and certainly luxuries, so he could rent space where he could write. All those stories about him only having space to write in his car are all part of a projected poor-me syndrome that adds to the drama of his success.

When we were in Sacramento, we had two salaries. He had his job in the hospital, and I was office manager at *Parents Magazine* Cultural Institute. My immediate supervisor there was Werner Erhard, who later founded *est*. Werner and I were good friends and would fly around to major cities to give addresses at various hotels. I had this job that made lots of money, and Ray was working at the hospital at that time. Werner was manager of the San Francisco office, and I was manager of the Sacramento office. I had never made so much money in my life. I'd had two years of college by then, and because of the poverty and Ray's and my situation, I had to drop out of Sacramento State even though I was making straight *A*'s and almost through with the semester; then the cookie thing came up and there was no money. I went around with tears running down my cheeks when I checked out of all my classes, and I went to work as a barmaid to pay everybody. The lights were turned off at our house at one time; and then, when we couldn't pay the rent, I took the children and went to my mother's in Paradise, California, and Ray had to go live with his parents. That was a real low point in the fall of '64 when we came back from Iowa. Then in January '65, I got the job at *Parents* and got out of the bar where I'd worked as a cocktail waitress—the first time I'd ever done that. At *Parents,* I just rose in the ranks. There was an opportunity to make money, dress well, use my intelligence; and I went for it. Before long I was wearing hundred-dollar dresses from Magnin's, and I had a maroon Pontiac convertible. We all started living the high life, you know. I knew in my heart that I would go back to college, that I really was a scholar; but it was such a relief for a while not to have this money worry. I felt like a thousand-pound weight had been lifted off my head.

That sounds like a relief, all right. What stopped it?

Well, Ray. *[Laughs.]* Ray did. He got jealous of my job and the power and attention I had there. Werner had told me to define the job I'd like to do. Of course, Werner and I were working with the materials that produced the foundation of the human-growth movement in California—in the world. We were right in there pioneering that, reading all the books— *Psychocybernetics, As a Man Thinketh, The Games People Play,* and all those.

You say Ray became jealous?

Well, there were these two handsome, brilliant men, Werner Erhard and Raymond Carver, in my life. One was my boss, and we'd go out to dinner and discuss business. I'd drive in my convertible that was faster than the wind, which I had thanks to my job, dressed in fancy clothes. In the meantime, Ray had this janitor job at the hospital— which was okay for him for a while as it meant security, and it gave him time to get a lot of writing done, but certainly no prestige associated with what he was doing. Werner thought it was a great idea when I defined my job as flying around to all the cities that had branches of this company and take employees out to cultural events to refresh them and give them another frame of reference. At that point Ray got a job as editor at SRA in Palo Alto, the first white-collar job he ever had. He then gave me an ultimatum—your marriage or your job. Werner and I didn't have a romance. It was just a work association—no hanky-panky whatsoever—but Ray decided to become head of the family with a vengeance just at that time.

I remember looking in the mirror and facing this enormous dilemma. I had to choose between a job I just loved or the man I loved. As it happened so many times when I had wonderful career opportunities, I had to turn them down because Ray and his career came first.

So after the ultimatum . . .

It was tough, because I was used to running an office, making good money, and now, all of a sudden—nothing. So I went back to college and eventually graduated from San Jose State, where I got my teaching credentials. I missed all the excitement of the job, but the thing I could always do was get *A*'s in school in everything.

So, to create some new excitement in my life, in the first semester at San Jose—this is spring '68 by now—I applied for a scholarship in the California State College Study Abroad program. They reviewed our application carefully; and it was just an incredible one, because Ray was a writer with all these publications to his credit, and yet we had these two children, so it would take a lot more money for a family to go abroad for a year than just a single student. Ours was a special and complex situation; so they made an exception, and we were accepted as a family. We were finally going to get to travel, which is what we had wanted for years and years to do.

Well, we were incredibly excited—high as kites. I was such a good student, that we had our choice to go anywhere—Uppsala, Sweden; or Florence, Italy; or Tel Aviv, Israel. Now as I view my grand life design, I see Israel was the absolutely perfect place for me, given my later interest in spiritual realities. To have had the opportunity at that age to go to the Holy Land was astounding planning on a higher plane when I think of how my life has gone since that time. We went there because *[laughs]* we were offered an extra five hundred dollars. Later Ray regretted we hadn't gone to Florence, because of his interest in the Renaissance and the art in that lovely city.

What was it like for Ray in Israel?

We only stayed four months. We were supposed to stay a whole year. Ray and my daughter both became very disgruntled. My son and I loved it. Ray had been publishing a lot of stories and poems just before we left. He was very eager to travel; but when we got over there, he'd say, "I don't know what I'm doing in Asia." We had an apartment which was small by our standards—only two bedrooms—but actually we had the apartment of the conductor of the Israel Philharmonic. By Israeli standards, we had a very special place, with paintings and wonderful art objects in the apartment. But Ray would sit out on the balcony and clutch his copy of *Life on the Mississippi [laughs]*, and sit there muttering "America First, America First," which was pretty wild because this was 1968, and Robert Kennedy—who I had voted for—had been shot, and Martin Luther King had been shot, and all that was going on the college campuses—the rallies and so forth. But for us, the trip to Israel made us appreciate our country, right or wrong.

Given that, did you stay much longer in Israel?

Well, we had been promised a villa on the Mediterranean, but they decided to use that villa for twelve students. Ray resented that we didn't have the villa, and the children weren't in English-speaking schools as promised. The children went to school in the old Arab city of Jaffa, and it took about an hour and a half to get there with three bus transfers. One day a bomb went off in a wastebasket in the bus depot, killing six people, just fifteen minutes after our children were there. Ray was upset. He said, "This may be the high time of your life, studying at the university, learning Hebrew, and listening to Golda Meir speak, and dancing Jewish folk dances, but I'm going to take my children and go home." There again I was faced with another ultimatum—except he had lined up a cruise from Haifa to Venice, first class for the regular cruise fare, by telling them he was a writer and would write an article about them. He told me we would stop in Athens and all the Greek Islands, and we'd send the kids home first and travel through Europe. And we did do all that.

So after you returned home?

Ray wound up after a while teaching at Iowa. He had already taught at Berkeley and Santa Cruz and also received the Wallace Stegner fellowship at Stanford. His friends not only called him Running Dog at that point, but also called him Feather In The Wind. He kept his job teaching in Santa Cruz while teaching in Iowa and flew back and forth without either school knowing about it.

Now that's a no-no—

[Laughs.] Well, Ray did all the no-no's. He did what he wanted. He was a renegade.

When did Ray first show signs of his alcoholism?

When his drinking pattern changed. We had always drunk socially, and occasionally we did get drunk. We didn't know alcoholism was a disease. We'd drink at a weekend party, but it was always a safe thing, because we'd look out for each other. As I said, it was only on occasion, and when it happened we thought it was funny. We took care of each other and no harm done. It was only when he taught the first year at the university that his drinking habits changed.

Was this at Iowa or Santa Cruz?

Santa Cruz. This was after we came back from Israel. I was teaching at Los Altos High School. The first year I taught, Ray had a whole year off where he could write, and he wrote many, many stories. He finished the bulk of *Will You Please Be Quiet, Please?*

What year was this?

That was in 1971. Ray was, to begin with, essentially a very shy person and introverted. Of course, once he got to know people, and with friends, he was different. *Will You Please Be Quiet, Please?* wasn't published until 1976, and for five years Ray didn't draw a sober breath. He left his job at University of California, Santa Barbara, a semester early due to his health, and after that he wasn't able to work until 1978.

How did you get by?

I had to support everybody—get up at six in the morning. We had to sell our house—*[She stops to draw a few deep breaths. We take a break.]*

Let's try it this way. Could you tell us more about when Ray started drinking heavily, and perhaps what you consider may have been the cause?

As I said, his drinking habits changed when he started to teach. He

95

was very shy. He had gone back to Iowa, before he taught at Santa Cruz, in the summer of '67 to study to be a librarian, because he liked libraries. He liked quiet little cubicles where he could work with books and magazines. Dick Day and some of his other friends wrote letters of recommendation, and he was accepted to get his master's degree in Library Science. But shortly after he started in that program, his father died, and Ray had to come back to California to bury his father, and so he got away from that. Then when he began to teach, it was a whole different thing. To be up in front of a class or group of people was terrifying for him. It was against his nature, though he became very good at it.

I had cooked up this teaching job for him through friends who knew James B. Hall, the provost of the program called *College V*, based on the Oxford system of individual colleges. Ray was flattered to get the job, but he would drink the moment he got out of class. He'd have several drinks, and his whole drinking pattern changed. He drank around his job, although he did an excellent job there. He put out a college magazine and worked with a group of good young writers.

How long did that last?

Well, the following summer, in 1972, Ray took a trip to Montana. He knew Bill Kittredge by then, and on this trip he made contact with a group of writers in Montana who did a lot of drinking. We always used to joke about how when Ray would go up there to visit, he was amazed to see that these men got up and showered and shaved and put on fresh starched shirts and dressed up at eight in the morning as if they were going off to work, when what they were doing was going off to drink.

Didn't you accompany him on these trips?

Yes, I went up there with him once; but he'd go without me, as I had my teaching job by then.

Did you look upon them as a drinking crowd?

Yes, and people who were divorced, and into their second and third wives and so forth. The slogan was another wife, another life. Remember, this was the seventies. There was a lot of disillusionment—the me-first generation. Women's lib came into flower; women were wanting divorces. Ray and I seemed like the last holdouts. We were ridiculed by all sorts of people because we were still together—high-school sweethearts. The other writers would say, "This reminds me of my first marriage." These were people now on their third or fourth, and they were great authorities with a couple of novels published. I'm not going to name names, but they were taking scenes from our life and putting them into their novels, making a satire of our lives. They'd say, "Get a divorce and grow." They were into a much wilder lifestyle than we'd ever had. And hanging out with this crowd, Ray became hopelessly addicted to alcohol.

Wasn't Ray writing from his experience about men having a problem holding on to their liquor, their marriages, their jobs?

People get into such generalities. Ray was a fiction writer. His work is not strictly autobiographical. Many incidents happened that were kernels of stories, but he had the dramatic sense to make them into a story that people would sit up and notice. The fact is that all happy families are alike, as Tolstoy observed, but unhappy families are unhappy in a unique way. Ray fastened on what was unhappy and unique in a situation and was able to create a dramatic story rather than a bland tale with no tension. A lot of times, as I've said, he'd take a kernel of something that really happened and convert it into a fine story.

Could you give us an example?

Well, take "Will You Please Be Quiet, Please?" That came out in 1967, just before we went to Israel, and was chosen for the Martha Foley collection of best American short stories of that year. I have an original copy upstairs in my bedroom. When that story came out, people were outraged or titillated to know just what the real situation had been. We'd go to parties and everybody was looking at me, and some would ask me, but I simply said that I'll never tell. It was important for Ray's career and his stories for me not to tell. It was rude of them to ask if it really happened or not. We knew that stories are stories.

Or take the story, "Are These Actual Miles?" I actually went out and sold my Pontiac convertible. It was my car, and I sold it, but how I sold it was nobody's business. Ray's story wasn't life. It was his story from an incident in our lives that captured his imagination, and Ray wrote it.

I know Ray created art out of life, but I always thought that particular story was especially close to his experience. The narrator is drinking heavily—

You know, Ray's father was an alcoholic; his grandfather was an alcoholic. They both died indirectly of alcoholism, and nobody ever said alcoholism. It wasn't recognized as a disease, as people look upon it today. Ray was around enough drinkers and mill workers to know about people who drink too much. It was not *us* in 1967 when he wrote a story. We did do some recreational drinking in Sacramento, but it wasn't the wild out-of-control drinking of the events after he started teaching at Santa Cruz. There was never a serious problem with alcohol before.

And then when it became a problem?

When it became a problem, he couldn't write. No stories were written when he was desperately drunk. He wrote those stories about people drinking when he was sober. It's how it was.

As I sit here listening to you, I cannot help thinking of the woman narrating Ray's story "Chef's House"—

Yes, I lived with Ray in Chef's house, but what happened wasn't exactly like the story. There are resemblances, of course. He was happy. I was still wearing my wedding ring, for example. What really happened in Chef's house was that at Christmas time he saw John Cheever on the Dick Cavett show. He had been friends with and drunk with Cheever back in Iowa, and here was his friend Little John and Dick Cavett talking about being a writer in New York. Ray made the decision to go east and be a writer there, and did so in January when he went back east to Goddard College. He uprooted the Chef's house to follow the route of John Cheever, whom he saw on a TV show. He had been sober since June of 1977, and by December he was ready to go. That's what happened at Chef's house. Also, Ray was writing well again in "Chef's House." He wrote "Why Don't You Dance?" and "Viewfinder" there, for example. He felt well by Christmas.

Not exactly the same as the story, was it?

No, Chef didn't take his house back to give to his daughter, for example.

Bankruptcy appears in many of Ray's stories and poems. Was that close to your experience?

Well, we did get into debt in Sacramento. It was a debt we had been paying, and I expected to continue making the payments. Ray got tired of that and suggested bankruptcy. We had a major disagreement about that. I was adamantly opposed to it—adamantly, adamantly, adamantly opposed to it.

Ray made that clear enough in those stories and poems. Why were you so opposed?

It wasn't my upbringing. My family upbringing was different. My family were teachers and landowners. My mother was a teacher.

Ray's story "Intimacy": What was your reaction to the emotion and sentiment expressed by the narrator to his ex-wife, begging her forgiveness?

It's difficult to say. *[Pause.]* The truth of it is I loved Ray Carver—first, last, and always. From the moment I met him until right now. There's no ending to that ever—and he felt the same about me. I learned from Ray. I knew how to live it unconsciously, but I learned as a concept from Ray what unconditional love really is. He'd say, "I love you whether you're good or bad." And indeed he did. And I loved him whether he was good or bad, even though there's no doubt I went through absolutely incredible grief over him. For years afterward I was truly heartbroken.

In modern psychological terms you're forced to say that no one hurts you. You allow someone to hurt you, and therefore you have to take responsibility for your own feelings. From that criteria, I can't say that he hurt me, although for years I felt he did. I did not feel I had a real choice about whether or not I was going to be hurt. It was a visceral response that almost overwhelmed me. God knows—and I am beginning to—he had his share of grief and suffering, too, despite the fame and fortune that came to him.

I was in so deep in that relationship—and he was, too—that pat cliches don't cut it. . . . We'd been in it forever. I met the love of my life when I was fourteen years old, for God's sake; and it takes a story like "Intimacy" to say what the psychologists merely hint at. Our emotions were so real, and raw, and overwhelming; we strongly affected each other always, together or apart.

What was your reaction to his success when it finally came?

After *Will You Please Be Quiet, Please?* was nominated for the National Book Award, and all those reviews came out in *Newsweek* and *Time* and all the press, it was a shock to me. Of course, it was exactly all that we had always prayed for, what we had worked so hard for, sacrificed for; but the fact of the matter was that it was tough to read those reviews and see your lives held up and analyzed. Characters were called inarticulate members of the working class, involved in violence and doomed to go nowhere. And again, there was such a mix-up between what is your real life and what is fiction because he did have He and She and their two children, a boy and a girl, over and over again in those stories. I found these classifications very difficult, because I had such great pride in Ray and his work and the hard work I had done and the things I had accomplished.

We had become beautiful people. We had developed, before the great fall, into people of enormous style and promise. We were also good people—hospitable and charitable people. All our friends came and stayed with us. Our families came. We believed in Homeric hospitality. We worked hard and it did pay off. All of a sudden, after many years of struggle, we did own a lovely home. We were both teachers. We did have enough income. Then when everything was in place, and the great challenge was gone, all that we had worked so hard for was knocked down. *[Pause.]*

You were saying that all you had worked for had been knocked down—

I read that book again with new eyes after all the reviews came out. I felt as if I were in a fishbowl and yet not really seen. Life was different than it had been before anybody knew us, and our lives had not been held up to review. Ray, of course, could not be blamed for what reviewers said; and I had always loved everything he wrote, starting with the first love poem he ever wrote for me. I always knew he was going to be a great writer, and I insisted on that. All the time he was drinking, I'd tell him that it would be the worst catastrophe that could ever happen, if he ended up as a second-rate writer, because we always agreed that he would be up there with the very, very best.

But convoluted as all this difficult part is—after the reviews, drunkenness, tensions, and separation—I then would read many of Ray's stories and poems, especially the later ones, with a very thin skin when I'd see how the lady or the son and daughter were done in for his capital gain. When *Fires* came out, for example, one of my son's professors was so concerned for him, knowing him to be a hardworking student and affable person, that he took Vance to lunch and tried to comfort him and explain what poetic license was all about. The kids, God bless them, have wonderful senses of humor and absolutely adored their father, again whether he was bad or good.

I know Ray did what he needed to do to write captivating stories and poems; profit, personal catharsis, and hurt to family members were secondary considerations at best. It is just that, privately, he was so decent and loyal. When he'd talk to me on the phone or write me letters, he would treat me with the utmost respect and love. I was the mother of the children, and if they needed anything, we worked on it together. We were a family—an unusually close family, all of us being basically as sensitive as flowers.

So if anything came out in print that was less than complimentary—less than real or true—I'd be very hurt and shocked by what felt like a real betrayal. Yet we'd both long before given up our personal selves for his literature. I had to lose my life to gain my life, so to speak. Looked at one way, Lenny Michaels was right. We did pay for those stories with our lives. Ray is dead, and I've lost my identity.

And about that story, "Intimacy," God bless Ray. He wrote whatever came to him; and if he could use anything, he did. I became super-sensitive as to how I was depicted on the page. But now, as I look back, I see Ray did not hesitate to portray himself either, in any position, humiliating or not. But he was a man and could get away with it better. He was also a star. He had a voice. I truly have been quiet, thank you. After all, what does it matter if Ray Carver humiliates himself? He doesn't really. He *is* Ray Carver.

May I say that whenever he wrote about the woman who may be construed as you, it never seemed to me to be condescending in any way.

Thank you. I didn't used to think so. I never did when we were together. I could read between the lines. He was captivated by me, first, last, and always. He used to say to me that I was absolutely dazzling. And anything negative, even in the last works—well, I *know*, in my heart of hearts, he did protest too much.

I read him as sympathetic to nearly all the women in his stories. They seem to be suffering for the shortcomings of their men.

Yes, Ray loved and understood women, and women loved him. Women know when a man really cherishes them or is just on a macho pursuit. Ray was sympathetic and lovable, and women adored him.

You've said that you and Ray kept communicating even after you and he had separated. Were you able to keep in touch up to the last stages of his illness?

Yes . . . during the last year he was especially very real, very open— no posing. He made every word, every feeling count. The last time I saw him alive was at the end of April 1988 when he was receiving radiation treatment in Seattle. Chris, our daughter, and her little girls, Windy and Chloe, and I went down to see him. I had received a letter from him earlier, right after he'd had his surgery, where he had tried to counsel me and advise me how to behave, consolidate property, and so on, now that we were sort of over the hill. When I read that, I thought, well, speak for yourself. I'm in the middle of all these projects, and I am working very hard. I'm young at heart and have always been an optimist. I was very saddened to read that negative letter, for, after all, I thought, that was not the right attitude to fight cancer with.

So I determined, when I went down to The Four Seasons in Seattle, where he was taking us all to lunch, that I'd show him. So I got this absolutely stunning outfit from this store in town, called A Touch Of Class, and wore these incredible gold earrings from Turkey that four people in the restaurant complimented me on. A friend said I looked like I'd just stepped out of a Ferarri.

We arrived before he did, so I waited for him up on the balcony, and when he walked in, oh *[sighs]* it was the most tragic sight I had ever, ever, ever seen. I saw him—his features—only in the middle of his face, it was so swollen. He had this big coat on, and a scarf around his neck, and a cap to cover his loss of hair from the radiation treatments. I saw him, and he saw me. He looked at me and tears flooded his eyes, and he said, "If you're not a sight for sore eyes."

But then he managed to put on a real party for the little girls. He was cheerful at lunch and insisted we all have a different dessert. We were a family, thrilled to be together, holding hands as we ate. They all looked at me at the beginning of the meal, so I said grace. I finished by saying "in Jesus' name." At one time, he would have been upset, but he was right in there this time. This was just gorgeous, because Ray was a consummate survivor. If praying would help now, he would pray. When we were together and we'd land in some God-forsaken little room temporarily, and I'd ask him jokingly how he could ever survive in this place, he'd pull a little can out of his pocket of roast beef hash, or whatever, and prepare a lunch for us. He was always going to survive, no matter what; and I took heart to see him pray with such gusto. I told him it was important to pray in Jesus' name, because it was the consciousness involved and invoked, as well as the literal instruction of Jesus in the Bible. I said a prayer for his life and health, and we all said Amen.

Then we had such a joyous lunch.

Can you remember the date?

April 22, 1988. He was totally, totally honest and real that day—his absolutely sweetest self. He paid us all compliments—compliments meant to last forever. Later that afternoon, I gave him a Reiki treatment. He would have scoffed at that, too, in the past and considered it an idiosyncrasy of mine. Reiki in the first degree is the laying on of hands technique that Jesus used to heal. It was discovered by a Japanese Christian professor after many years of research. Ray laid his head on the palms of my hands. My hands got hot, and I was holding the exact part of his head where he was daily being zapped with radiation treatments. And he absolutely loved lying with his head in my lap, his head in my hands. He kept saying, "This feels so good; oh, this feels so good!"

Were you in touch with him at all after that time?

Yes, he called me on our anniversary in June. He wrote me many letters. He sent me books. He sent me this copy of *Where I'm Calling From. [She gets a book from the dining room table covered with many pieces of Carver memorabilia.]*

Looking back on it all, what would you say about Ray now?

I think Ray did his job in this life. He honored his life goal and became a first-rate writer who is cherished and read all over the world. I am so proud of him and so pleased with his success. I appreciate the care that Tess gave him that last year, and the other help she gave him in his career and his life. Against many odds, but with many boons and lots of love and support, he realized his talent and accomplished his dream.

On a superficial level, he did not want to die, of course. But I think he had written out all his themes and didn't have a whole lot more to say, or he would have stuck around to do it. I think his Higher Self knew when it was time to go—at the very pinnacle of his life, as far as his career was concerned. Ray always had a short attention span. He could never stand to be bored. He liked to move on, even from ostensibly good situations. I think, on some higher plane, he wanted to move on and do something else.

And always, from the day I met him, he knew he was going to

die young. We always deferred to what he wanted to do because, however tacitly, we both feared he did not have a long time on this earth.

For instance, the last ten years of his life: after five treatment centers, he was sober. After a sick and shaky start, he was writing again as well as ever. At that juncture I checked out and let him have his life, to experience all he could, because he was forty then, and who knew how long he had. He always said, "I'm going to die young, but you're going to live to be a mean old lady."

Ray had a great spirit. He was overall a wonderful husband and father; and there were always more smiles than tears. And I have no doubt in my mind or heart—that bottom line—neither one of us would have missed it for the world.

And, of course, looked at another way, we ended up having it, too . . .

September 13, 1990
Blaine, Washington

*Richard Ford, Raymond
Carver, Toby Wolff, and
Geoffrey Wolff on
Geoffrey's boat.*

GEOFFREY WOLFF

Ray understood that questions and answers are in some way combative, and he mastered this understanding that every question is loaded in some way with menace and consequence. Every question seems to be binary. You have two roads you can go down, and the answer you choose can change your life. The smallest matters can have the gravest consequences.

I meet Geoffrey Wolff for the interview in his office at Brandeis University in Waltham, Massachusetts. It is a small room—about eight by ten feet, cement block walls, one window, one desk, two chairs—bare and functional as a shoebox. A dozen or so photographs of Wolff's family and his boat are neatly displayed on a pair of wooden boards supported by hardware store brackets meant to serve as bookshelves.

He is eating a tuna fish sandwich at his desk when I come in. He smiles and waves an arm in amiable greeting, and I see a remarkable physical resemblance to his brother, Tobias. He is a cheerful man, affable, and easy to talk to. We take turns passing on stories about Ray and his escapades. The conversation and ideas flow so spontaneously that I rush to hook up my tape recorder. I don't want to waste any of this good stuff.

Sam Halpert: Where and when did you first meet Ray Carver?

Geoffrey Wolff: I met Ray for the first time in Vermont at the Goddard College M.F.A. writing program. It was very shortly after he had stopped drinking, and so it was the first job that he'd had after he had pulled himself together. We made an immediate friendship. The person who introduced me to him was my brother, Toby, who had met Ray shortly before I did. I went to Goddard to give a reading and in no time at all we were laughing. Ray was a great laugher, and we sat around telling outrageous stories to each other.

Love at first sight. How do you account for it?

Ray was the first writer I had met who made me conscious that anything I said to him he would take as his property, and that was something I was perfectly willing to surrender for the pleasure of his company. So my first memory was of an extraordinary listener and an extraordinary user.

Was this in the winter of '78, the same time that your brother Toby wrote about in his wonderful memorial essay on Ray?

Yes, and there's a great story about Ray from that year. He was having a hard time financially just then. When he was given the Goddard job, a couple of his friends—Michael Ryan was one of them—had to make guarantees that Ray would be okay to teach and behave himself. Ray came ready to teach, though he was pretty shaky. He was in rough shape physically, but he had an atmosphere of resolve about him. As you know, each teacher at Goddard is assigned five students to supervise. Well, shortly after he left, it turned out that Ray had gone to some of his students and borrowed fifty to a hundred bucks from them—paid it back, too, which was a new habit for him.

You said that he'd take what you said as his property. Can you recall anything you said that became a Carver story?

Oh, no. It wasn't a question of getting a story from me. It's a phrasing, a sense of observation, a kernel here and there. But, of course, we all do this. You don't know anything until you hear it. But with Ray, you were *conscious* of his attention, that he was making stories all the time, shaping them, figuring how to make them track. He loved to hear stories. I never knew anyone who was a better audience.

How was he at telling stories?

He could really tell a story. I remember he told a story once in Provincetown. He was in residency there, and I came to give a reading. I was there with Richard Ford and his wife, and my wife, and Ray was there with his son. Ray told us a story I had never heard before. It was about the time he was in Israel on a fellowship. He had his choice of Tel Aviv or Florence, Italy, but Tel Aviv paid five hundred dollars more, and that's all he needed to know. In the story, he put his kids in Hebrew-speaking schools that neither he or they understood, and they lived in some squalid walk-up tenement, and he used to take a bus across town to buy fish. He'd come back on the bus with this bucket of fish. Well, the story was so graphic; it had art and geography in it. It had a character change, and motive, all *ad hoc*. And centered in this story was this bucket of fish on a crowded bus, and people staring at it. And the way the whole story started was somebody mentioned whitefish.

From what I hear, Ray was none too happy in Tel Aviv.

You see, I didn't meet Ray until after he stopped drinking, so all I know of his unhappiness was the great joy we all took in the narratives that came out of it. Ray had good luck. Ray had bad luck. He was an alchemist in the way he could turn the worst squalor into the best stories. So when I think of the bad old days for Ray, what I see are the wonderful stories.

How did you keep in touch with Ray?

We saw each other at Goddard; we corresponded. He came to see me and Richard Ford when I was teaching at Princeton. I saw him in Arizona with my brother, Toby. We kept in touch, visited, and I was very much in touch with his work. I had the luck to be asked by the *New York Times* to review a collection of stories. I told them I had given up reviewing, but they said I might be interested in this book and they sent it on to me. It turned out to be *Will You Please Be Quiet, Please?* This was before I had met Ray. I saw those stories, and I don't think I was more than three sentences into the first story before I knew I was hearing a voice I had never heard before. So I was disposed to feel strongly about Ray before I met him.

What did you hear in that voice?

First of all, you can't talk about his fiction without talking about the speed of his beginnings. Ray propels you into his world fast and without tricks. It's his absolute solid-rock belief in the world he is describing, along with a master's understanding of voice. So you get propelled into his world sensually, and into the grammar of this world. Dumb-headed critics seem to pay attention to what kind of house Ray's people are living in, what kinds of clothes they're wearing, and all that. I don't think this has anything to do with his stories. They live by their sound and syntax, his bravura abbreviation, the speed and indirection of the narrative. And in all these things, he is a great master of grammar.

Did you say grammar?

I say grammar rather than diction, because the *words* don't arrest or surprise me so much. It's their wonderful loopiness. I think Ray was able to make the same revolution in his own way that Harold Pinter made.

    For example, he understood questions; how they can be menacing. Ray understood that questions and answers are in some way combative, and he mastered this understanding that every question is loaded in some way with menace and consequence. Every question seems to be binary. You have two roads you can go down, and the answer you choose can change your life. The smallest matters can have the gravest consequences.

You mentioned the speed in which the reader is immediately—"propelled," I believe is the word you used—into a Carver story. Could that be because we understand so much of what has happened to the characters even before the story begins?

That's a good question. There's always something in the beginning that throws you a little off guard, because Ray was a master at locating a moment that would change people's lives.

Just to pursue this a little further—in the story "So Much Water So Close To Home," so much has happened before the story begins—

This is so, but they're all different. In "Gazebo," for example, "That morning she pours Teachers over my belly and licks it off." And in "Viewfinder," "A man without hands came to the door to sell me a photograph of my house." In "What We Talk About When We Talk About Love" there's the slow unfolding of the story.

It wasn't only in his beginnings.

Yes, he's also a master of titles. And if he's somewhere now eavesdropping, I'm sure he won't mind my saying that he used to run a bit of a scam when he'd be asked to deliver a lecture on the craft of fiction. He used to have one that he'd pull out of his back pocket. It was a lecture on titles. He'd give a little rap on the importance of titles. He and I gave a team lecture once and he said, "When you see a house, the first thing you see is the roof, right? The roof is everything." Well, I looked at him and questioned whether that was the way it works. So he said, "Okay, it's the chimney. The first goddamn thing you see is the chimney." When I questioned that, Ray said, "Well then, it's the front door. This is the title. You go through the front door and you're into your story."

When I asked him for an example of a favorite title of his own, he gave me "What We Talk About When We Talk About Love."

Speaking of titles, I remember asking Ray to name his favorite short story. That's dumb-ass, I know, but I asked it. He told me you could learn a lot from "Hills Like White Elephants," the Hemingway story. Maybe he was just dusting me off, but I read the story again, and when I came to the part where the girl says, "Will you please please please please please please please be quiet," I knew where Ray got his title.

Oh, if it was good, he'd take it from anywhere. In that story, too, there was something that Ray was a master of. He knew better than anyone where his characters should look. I don't mean point of view. I mean where their eyes fall—what they see and what they don't see. I think he learned a lot from "Hills Like White Elephants" when the characters look at each other, and away from each other, and at their hands, at their feet, at the table. Ray was a master of where eyes fall, where they rest. *[Pause.]*

Would you like to hear some fishing stories about Ray?

I've heard a few; but, sure, tell me yours.

Well, I have two fish stories. One of them is from when my wife met him for the first time. She fell in love with him—everyone did; you'll hear that over and over again; that's the way he was. Anyway, her heart just opened to him. We were up in Vermont, and he said he was going out to do some fishing. She asked him if he were a fly fisherman. And he said that he was a fly fisherman if the fish were taking the fly; otherwise he used blasting caps.

The other story is when my son and I and Tess and Ray were in Alaska together. We rented a car and went off to find a river where we could fish for Arctic grayling. In Vermont, you only have to go a couple of miles to find a good trout stream, but we had to drive over forty miles to find a place to fish in Alaska. And when we got there— out in the boonies in Alaska, in the middle of the tundra—there must have been fifty or sixty cars there. Well, on top of that, it was raining. Tess stayed in the car. She wasn't that stupid. But I was that stupid, and my son, Nicholas, and Ray was that stupid, so we got out of the car to fish. Ray was giving all kinds of instructions to Nicholas on fishing. And after a while Nicholas got a bite. Ray started on Nicholas to pass over the rod to him. And Nicholas said that it was okay, he could handle it himself. But Ray kept after him and tried to take the rod; but Nicholas wouldn't let him. Pretty soon it was like Ray's story where they tear the baby apart.

He loved to see other people catch fish, too. He always thought it was magic. Ray would say it like a litany, and you knew it was coming. "Goddamn it, aren't we lucky. Aren't we lucky," he'd say. He'd say it over catching a fish or anything that happened. And in the years I knew him, he was lucky, he was blessed. I don't believe I ever saw anybody with such an alive awareness and appreciation of life.

What's your reaction to the criticism of him as a minimalist?

I'll make one comment off the bat. The comment has been well considered, and the scholarly term for the comment is bullshit. I'm not sure I know what a minimalist is. I kind of think I know what people mean when they say they think they know what a minimalist is—that it is a taker-outer rather than a putter-inner. And to a certain degree, Ray was that. He liked to lean things down, but not always. He was certainly capable of being a putter-inner too. Ray wrote enough. It was a wonderful thing that Stanley Elkin, who is certainly no minimalist, said. He said that he didn't understand what this less-is-more crap was about. He said, "Less is less. More is more. And enough is enough." And Ray was someone who knew what enough was. Now there was a time when the stories that are collected in *What We Talk About When We Talk About Love* were being screwed down— some of them maybe a little too tight, you could say that—and I think Ray came to think this. As you know, when he revised those stories, he filled them out a bit, but I think not always wisely.

I think "Mr. Coffee and Mr. Fixit," for example, in its leaner version is a better story than "Where Is Everyone?"—the version he expanded and put in *Fires.* Certainly stories like "Cathedral" and "Errand" are not minimal. There are people who are tricksters, hacks, workshop writers who think they are imitating Carver in the way they were imitating Hemingway in an earlier time. They've created an atmosphere of sparseness and niggardliness, and there's no sense of life beneath the work. It's just lean and white space. But Ray wrote *enough.* His stories are full. As I say, there was a time when he was getting close to the edge; and in some instances not worth mentioning here, he actually did go over that edge. Yes, he came close to crossing the line, as actually "Hills Like White Elephants" comes close to crossing that line. It could be argued that there is insufficient information in that story. But this minimalist crap is not worth talking about any—

Ray wrote frequently, especially in his poems, about death. Did he ever speak to you about death?

No, no, and I mean no. We had one discussion once and it had nothing to do with literature. It was after I'd had a heart operation, and it was shortly before Ray found out that he was sick. I had written something about this operation and the events leading up to it. And, very characteristic of me, the seriousness in that piece came from what I hoped was a comic imagination. I don't believe I can be accused of solemnity. So Ray had taken some pleasure from the piece, but when I spoke to him about the origin of the piece and explained some of the details of the illness, it was the only time I ever noticed him uneasy around me. He did not want to talk about bad luck or bad news. The subject of illness or death was not at all welcome. On the page, it was a different matter, but not face to face.

I'm sure you spoke to him after he discovered he had cancer. What was the scope of those conversations?

I had several conversations with him after he found out. He was going to have an operation at one point that was similar to one I'd had, and I wanted to tell him as much as he wanted to know about that particular operation. He asked me some questions about it, but he told me, going in, exactly what he did not want to know about it. I know I'd want to know all I could—after all, knowledge is power. But not Ray. He wanted, as he said, to wake up three months later and find out it was all fixed, that it was all over.

Would you call it denial?

No, although I think Ray was perfectly capable of denial. I'd say it was more that Ray believed in the power of language so profoundly—it was so sacred to him—that he understood as few people understand that words are loaded pistols. Sometimes to say something, to name it, is to enact it. So there were certain words he would not say.

Did you attend the funeral service for Ray in Port Angeles?

No, I was out of the country at the time, but I heard about it.

What did you hear about it?

Oh, that emotions were running very high. I believe the thing I would like to say about what I heard was that the way I understand Ray was laid out for viewing was a scene that only Ray himself could have done justice to in a story—a story that would have been peculiarly Carver-like in its plangence, sadness, and high comedy. The scene of the open display of the body was something that he as a great writer could have appreciated. That's about as much as I care to get into here.

Okay. Ray wrote so many, but which of his stories did you personally favor—and, perhaps, tell us why?

Well, I do have a couple, and they come from different periods. We were talking before about "Why Don't You Dance?" What I admire most about that story is, again, the extraordinary speed in which you perceive the lives of the young, callow couple. Then you see her deepen right in front of you. At the end of the story, there are two lightning-fast changes of direction. At the very end, when she calls him the poor old guy, or something like that, and she tells the story of this old guy with all his furniture out there in his front yard. Then her mood darkens and she realizes it's her life, too, the culmination of her life—that we're all in the same boat. I like that story.

"What We Talk About When We Talk About Love" I admire so much because, first of all, I don't think there has ever been anything even approximately as good written about drinking. I've done enough drinking in my life to know how it feels, what happens to syntax, what happens to diction, as the light begins to come down in the room and the stuff goes further down in the bottle. The room darkens, and you see your whole life darken too. The only other writer who can do that kind of story is Cheever. Cheever stories do have that kind of quality.

But the two stories that absolutely knock me off my pins are "Cathedral," which surprised me—that story takes a turn I never anticipated, although I knew Ray's heart was capacious enough to have written a story like that. It was a daring story—perhaps the most touching story, for me, that he had written. I think it shows extraordinary skill—Ray always had skill—but this story has an emotional precision, a predictable willingness to surrender to strangeness. The whole situation is so strange. But, brilliantly, the emotional relationship between the narrator and the blind man becomes so direct and so *uneccentric* (which may be the word I'm looking for) and so credibly human. It's us at our best—people at their best.

Then there's the story that if it didn't teach me something about writing, there's something wrong with me; and that's "Errand." I remember reading it in *The New Yorker*—reading about the death of Chekhov—and I'm a biographer as well as a novelist, and it starts out, as you know, as a conventional biography about the last days of a great man. I thought I understood what was happening, and I was puzzled by it. It took a bit of patience, because I was finding it almost tedious at the beginning. I didn't know where he was going with this story. Then after Chekhov has died and the waiter comes on, all disheveled, waiting for his tip, and spots the champagne cork lying on the rug and steps on it so they won't notice it, I realized then where Ray's eye had been all during that story. His eye had been on the guy no one ever notices, standing offstage, and he's the most important character in the story. I was deeply affected by that. I realized how many of us have had our eyes on the wrong characters. Ray had something to teach us, and he did.

It's curious that you should focus on that aspect of Ray's writing. When I asked your brother, Toby, for a characteristic example of Ray's writing, he chose the poem, "The Baker," the one about Pancho Villa and Count Vronsky taking over this Mexican baker's house and wife, and waving pistols around. The poem ends with this little baker sneaking off barefoot, in fear of his life. Ray writes that he, the baker, is the hero of this poem. All along we've been looking at Vronsky and Villa, which is just about the same point you make about "Errand."

You said earlier that everybody seemed to love Ray. What did you find in him most engaging?

It's probably important to say right here, to keep this in perspective, that Ray was a great liar, a wonderful liar. I'll tell you a story about that. I have a sailboat. Ray, Richard Ford, my brother, Toby, and I went out on the boat over to Block Island. Richard and my brother and I went ashore to do some drinking. Of course Ray couldn't be interested in that. So we left him aboard, and he wanted to know where the coffee was. I told him the stove was pretty complicated and it could easily blow up, and I'd bring him back some coffee because I didn't want him to use the stove. I gave him my orders on that. And he said, " Oh, Jesus, I wouldn't dream of touching that stove. I don't truly need the coffee that much anyway." I told him again if he wanted any, I'd be glad to bring some back for him. He said no, he'd be all right. So we left him and went into town and somehow drifted into a bar. My brother wanted to talk about literature, and Richard and I wanted to talk about waitresses, which is what we were looking at there.

Pretty soon we thought it was time to go back to Ray, so we took one of the waitresses back with us to take our picture, and we got into the dinghy. When we got close, I noticed Ray was back in the stern of the boat, as far back as he could get, and he looked awful. As a matter of fact, what he looked like was very dirty. So I asked him what the hell happened. He said, "Don't worry about a thing. I've just been shooting smack into my eyeballs." I knew he was joking, but the waitress was terrified. I knew it was a joke and went below to get my camera. Now my boat is a beautiful boat, and below it used to be all white. But now it was black—soot everywhere. It was completely black. It took me and my son, Nicholas, ten years to scrape all that damn soot off. I was so mad. I said, "Jesus, Ray. Son of a bitch, you shouldn't have done that." He said, "What are you talking about? I didn't do a damn thing." I said, "Come on, Ray, you lit that stove. God, Ray, I told you to keep away from it." "I don't know what you're talking about," he said. "I was sleeping for a while. Maybe someone came aboard, but what are you talking about?" I told him to look down below. He said, "That's just the way it looked when you guys left." It took us ten years to finally scour that boat down clean.

Sometimes, like now, remembering Ray, I wonder if I shouldn't have left it the way it got that morning in the harbor at Block Island. Carvered.

October 3, 1990
Waltham, Massachusetts

Ray and Sappho the cat in
Kinder's and Cecily's flat
on California Street in
San Francisco, 1977.

CHUCK KINDER

Ray always said that you should trust the accidents in your work and, of course, in your life. In "Are You a Doctor?" suddenly there's a random telephone call—there are so many phone calls in Ray's work—out of the blue, a sudden telephone call that sets off a series of events that then take on a mysterious meaning. You don't know exactly what they mean—that's the mystery.

The interview is held in the kitchen of the sixteen-room, turn-of-the-century, yellow brick house in Pittsburgh where Chuck Kinder lives with his wife, Diane. Chuck always holds his long, serious conversations over kitchen tables wherever he lives. It comes from a warm, old-fashioned, country way of living. After the interview, I sit in on the writing class he teaches at the University of Pittsburgh and learn a thing or two about the art of fiction from this good ol' country boy.

Sam Halpert: Would you describe your first meeting with Ray?

Chuck Kinder: I don't remember when I first met him, but I know when he first made an impression on me. It was in '72 when we were at Stanford together. He had a Stegner fellowship and I had an Edith Mirrielees fellowship, and I must have met him the first day in workshop, but I don't remember. I'd seen him sitting around mumbling a lot, and smoking, and biting on his thumbnail. He'd make comments now and then on the other students' stories—not a lot of comments, but when he did, they were really astute. I was impressed with that.

How old was he then?

Oh, about thirty-four. He was a big shambling fellow—always wore shades. I thought he dressed goofy. He looked like someone who I'd take their lunch money away from when I was a kid. At any rate, one day I needed a ride down El Camino Real and I asked if anyone was going in that direction. Ray raised his hand and said he was going in that direction, and I said to myself, "Dear God, not this goofy guy."

Had you been avoiding him all this time?

Well, not exactly. You have to understand that those were the days when *The Whole Earth Catalog* was current. It was hip to be close to the earth and all that. Everyone was walking around wearing work boots and work clothes and since I came from West Virginia and I'd worked in a coal mine, I could affect that look with a little more authority.

And what was Ray wearing?

He looked like a big goofball. Corduroy pants. Shirts that he had buttoned up to the collar. Like he didn't care if he was cool at all. He looked like no one who'd interest me. And of course it turned out later that was wonderful, that he didn't think about bullshit like that. Anyway, I took him up on his offer of a ride and we went out to the parking lot. He had an old battered Mercury convertible that looked like it would fall apart even while we looked at it. Someone had dumped the ashtray all over the car floor. That car was full of crap—manuscripts, paper cups, cigarette butts everywhere.

And a load of unpaid parking tickets?

Oh, sure, all that. Then we had to pray that the car would start. It coughed and hacked and wheezed and bounced all over the lot. About that time a bottle slid out from under the seat, a bottle of very cheap scotch. And Ray looked down at it and said, "Ooh, look what we have here," laughing in that way of his. "How do you suppose this got here? Maybe we should have us a little drink. What do you think?" So I said, "Sure, why not? Let's have us a little drink." And he passed it over. I don't know what scotch it was. It tasted like hair tonic. It was about a half a quart, and he didn't have far to take me—just three miles down El Camino—but we pretty near killed it by the time he let me off. I thought this guy was a nut, and I didn't want him to know where I lived on Matadora Road, so I told him to let me off at the corner at the Taco Bell. He did, and he drove off in that old car, bouncing into the sunset looking like an accident waiting to happen. And I thought, that was the last time I'm going to have anything to do with him. It wasn't that I disliked the guy; it's just that I couldn't figure him out.

Sounds like you took him for some kind of nerd.

Yeah, he was a nerd. He wasn't a hip, red-necked good ol' boy like me at all.

Well, we know he wasn't a nerd and that it wasn't the last you saw of him. When did you see him next?

My first wife, Janet, and I lived in a little bungalow we rented from a woman whose father had built it by hand. She gave us a break on the rent for me to do the yardwork, which I never did. When she'd come to check things out, I'd be hiding inside with the curtains drawn and wouldn't answer the door. Well, about ten o'clock the next morning I heard a pounding on the door, and I thought it was the landlady. I got very quiet and turned off the TV, but the knocking kept on—rap, rap, rap—and finally I took a peek, and it was Ray with a pile of magazines and books in one arm and a bag in the other arm.

What was in the bag?

More magazines and a bottle of cheap booze and some ice. These were magazines he had stories in. At that time he had eight or nine stories published in magazines like *Quarterly West* and other small magazines. There he was, and I let him in.

There he was. Did he just want to hang out with you?

Yeah, he asked me if I was working on anything. And I told him to get serious; I was only watching TV. So we went out to the kitchen, sat down, had a drink, and started talking. He gave me copies of his stories he wanted me to read. I was pleased at that. I gave him a copy of my first novel that had just come out. I had finished it after my first year at Stanford, and thought I was pretty much of a hot shot. That may have been another reason I'd been snotty to him.

What was your reaction to his work after you read it?

I was amazed by it. I thought it was wonderful writing. It was spare; but what really impressed me then, as it continues to impress me now, is . . . I don't want to get into all this analysis of his work.

I'm sorry, Chuck, but I'm afraid we can't talk about Ray without talking about his work.

Well, what I liked then, and what I keep returning to now, and what I talk about to my classes—we always go over two or three of his stories every term, and always "Cathedral" because it epitomizes one of the things I really care about in writing—and that is the discovery of the mystery in the mundane. He could find the art in everyday occurrences. I read somewhere that early Christianity had such appeal because it made mystery democratic. It wasn't filtered down through priests. You could have mystery in your everyday life. In an amazing way, Ray did that with his work, in that strange conjunction between accident and art.

Did you recognize this in his work from the start?

Yes, especially in stories like "Are You a Doctor?" and "Put Yourself in My Shoes"—those stories. I liked the Kafkaesque quality in those stories: the way accidents happen that can determine your fate. Ray always said that you should trust the accidents in your work and, of course, in your life. In "Are You a Doctor?" suddenly there's a random telephone call—there are so many phone calls in Ray's work—out of the blue, a sudden telephone call that sets off a series of events that then take on a mysterious meaning. You don't know exactly what they mean—that's the mystery. You have to read Ray's work with the same intensity as you read poetry. Those stories, to my mind, sort of pointed toward what Flannery O'Connor talks about as a big mystery—the big mystery beneath the surface of the story. Especially in Ray's stories that had a mystery, there's a sense of a crafted meaning that glimmered under the surface of the story. At any rate, I always thought the title of his first collection should have been *Put Yourself in My Shoes*, but Gordon Lish insisted on *Will You Please Be Quiet, Please?* (which is a wonderful story, of course) and that's the way it went.

Let's go back to what happened after Ray's first visit to you back in Stanford.

Well, we started hanging out together, and a couple of nights later he brought Maryann over to meet my wife. We never actually did talk that much about writing, thank God. We'd be sitting around talking about events in our lives, and it would be interesting to see how he and Maryann would talk about horrific things they had gone through. Bill Kittredge has a terrific story about a couple of old funky barroom ladies who have learned to cut their losses to jokes. And that's what happened with Ray and Maryann. They'd tell these horrific stories and they'd be laughing about them. The stories took on a legendary tall-tale quality, and they'd embellish them as they went along.

It's interesting that, when Ray was drinking, he'd blank out a lot. His memory would be affected, and Maryann's wasn't. So very often Ray would question her, almost like an interview, asking, "Then what did I do after that?" I could see the story taking root in Ray's mind as Maryann would plumb her memory about events. That happened time and time again. So when you were with them, there was a sense of play—dangerous play, true—that they were amazed by and always trying to understand. But with all that booze, it got dark and evil toward the end—really destructive—and Ray couldn't handle it.

We're told there may be a genetic factor to alcoholism.

Oh, yes. Ray's father was an alcoholic. Alcohol acted as a sort of fuel for him. And, of course, he was basically very shy. It was interesting that so many of the things they did that make up all the Ray and Maryann stories and anecdotes, I could see them being created—not consciously, I'm sure—but as though they were trying to create a story to tell later. An accident would happen that would lead to another, and he would trust the accidents and sort of follow where they led, each moment having its own fan-shaped destiny. There was a certain childlike quality to all that, a strange sense of play. You'll see kids fighting and saying, "I hate you—I hate you." Then, a few minutes later, they're best friends again. We'd have situations when there'd be a shattering of glass and yells and screams and howls in the night, and the next minute they'd be ordering pizza. And then

Maryann would say, "Did you see what Ray just did?" and then tell the story as if it were all some kind of amazing game whose rules they were trying to discover after the fact. There was a hilarity to it, but that ultimately feeds on itself. The fiction devours itself.

Was all this while you were still at Stanford, in Palo Alto?

Yes, but they were living in Cupertino. As I said, my first wife and I and Ray and Maryann started running together. I remember one night we had to carry them home and literally put them in bed. Maryann was so impressed by that. She laughed and said their other friends would just dump them on the porch for their kids to find them in the morning.

Could you tell more about how they reacted to each other?

Sure. It was on their fifteenth or sixteenth wedding anniversary. Maryann was amazingly generous. Ray was generous, too, but when it came to money he could be a little tight. Ray and I had this relationship where we'd bicker a lot. You know, one-upmanship—like bickering brothers. Like, did you buy that last drink, or did I buy the last two? and all that business. Maryann, though, with her last penny would buy a turkey or a ham and throw a party for the whole neighborhood. So they came sweeping over to my house—they'd had a few, and were real high and funny. She invited Janet and me to go out and celebrate with them at a Greek restaurant. When we got there, Ray got upset with her. Obviously she had been to this restaurant before, and she wouldn't come clean as to who she'd been there with or why, and he was very suspicious. But at that point, Ray was involved with someone else; and Maryann was at the edges of some stuff also. So there was suspicion between the both of them. So we all were at this Greek restaurant, and it turned into a typical Carver story.

I remember they had a floor show, and they had a strong man who picked up tables with his teeth. At one point he did a backbend and invited people from the audience to come up and step on his stomach. His assistant took Ray by the hand and pulled him up there. Ray was laughing and saying, "Okay, okay." He stumbled and tumbled all over that strong man. One crazy thing after another. But as the evening wore on, Ray decided, since he was paying for it, that he couldn't afford any more. I was pegged out but kept ordering more drinks, more champagne. Ray was getting more irritated with me. He started sulking, saying, "We're not paying for him." After a while he decided that we'd walk the check. My wife had seen and heard enough. She was a real sweet straight-arrow and had seen enough of our silly act. She went out to the car to wait for us to settle the whole thing. She was the designated driver and we were the designated drunks all the time. The next thing I knew, Ray had disappeared. He was going to stick me with the check. I told Maryann that I had no money, no plastic, nothing. She had some plastic, but on more than a few occasions in the past their card had come back—a pitiful thing, cut in two on a tray, rejected. Maryann wasn't sure whether the plastic she had was good or not, so she told me to go out through the bar, and she would walk out slowly later. We were going to walk the check after all.

When I got out to the car, my wife was behind the wheel, engine going, and Ray was lying low, lurking in the back seat. Then Maryann came out, and just then our waiter came out and put his hand on Maryann's shoulder. Ray said to my wife, "Step on it—step on it!" He wanted to leave Maryann behind in the dust, anniversary or no anniversary. I talked some sense back into him. We went back into the restaurant, and Maryann was sitting at the bar giving the cashier her plastic. Ray was worried, asking her what they were going to do if it wasn't any good. Maryann said that she would then have to write them a check, which was a laugh. She had all the bravado in the world, and she could carry it off. She really had a flair. The plastic worked, thank God, and we got out of there.

After his year at Stanford, did he go up to Berkeley?

Yes, Lenny Michaels got him in there. Once Ray got me fifty bucks for reading to his class, and we drank it up at a hotel bar in Berkeley ahead of him. He wanted me to meet a girl in his class who had written a story about being gang-banged by a biker club. She had a crush on Ray, and he was frightened to death of her. He wanted me to meet her. She was a cute, tattooed chick. He introduced me to the class first as a panel, then as Truman Capote. We ended by driving up to Davis to see Jack Hicks, stopping at a bar on the way called Dutch's. One thing leads to another, and the alcohol acts as a fuel, and you could see the story happening. Nothing really happened with the girl—well, not much. But it got on the verge of crazy stuff. At one point we both decided we were in love with her. Anyway, we were living the story and knowing we were living it—first making it into a literary tall tale and then making it into a one-upmanship story that we would tell at a kitchen table. We spent a lot of time at kitchen tables batting stories back and forth, until the truth was just where we wanted it to be.

How long did he stay at Berkeley, and why did he leave?

He was teaching at Berkeley while he had his Stegner at Stanford. You weren't supposed to do that, but he was always pulling stunts like that. He'd send his stories out to a half-dozen magazines at once. That story, "So Much Water So Close to Home" was published in two separate journals before he sold it to *Playgirl*.

Did he make any revisions before he sent it out?

No, no—the same story.

Was it right about then when he worked up that deal where he was teaching at Iowa and Santa Cruz at the same time?

Yes, that's when he would teach at Iowa the beginning of the week and fly back to Santa Cruz to teach at the end of the week. That's when I met Bill Kittredge, who was down at Stanford on a Stegner. I don't know how many times Bill and I went up to teach Ray's class at Santa Cruz.

He sort of pulled this again later when he was teaching at Santa Barbara—only that time he was collecting unemployment checks from the state while he was working. He almost went to jail on that one, but Maryann saved his bacon. She got up in court and pled everything but her belly to get him on probation. It took Maryann, Kittredge, Max Crawford, and myself all to drag Ray down for the first meeting with his probation officer. We had to literally walk him to the door and shove him in.

Was this when you and your wife were still running around with Ray and Maryann?

No, this was later. My first wife and I had split up by then. I had been on leave from Stanford, where I was by then a Jones lecturer, when my first wife justifiably parked me at the curb, and I had nowhere to go; so Bill Kittredge offered me a little spot up in Missoula. Ray and Maryann were having trouble, because he was deeply in love with another woman who he had been involved with for a couple of years. Maryann had found a pack of letters from this woman, so Ray gave me some stuff to take back for safekeeping to this woman when I went back to Montana to live with Bill. That's where this woman lived. I met her and gave her the stuff from Ray. That was Diane, my present wife. I fell madly in love with her. I felt bad about Ray, but he had his chance. He had broken promises with her for years. He hadn't left Maryann and it looked like he never would. When Kittredge went back to Stanford and told Ray, he said that Ray was real pissed at me. Ray said that we always called *him* Running Dog, but Kinder was the real running dog.

How did you make up?

Ray phoned one day and we talked it all over, and when the conversation was over we were laughing. He was calling me names like back-stabber and asshole and all that. You'd think it would affect our friendship, but it didn't. When Diane and I moved back down to Palo Alto before we moved to San Francisco, Ray had moved back in with Maryann, and we all went out together; and we were closer as couples than we had been when I was married to my first wife.

A good friend, Scott Turow, who was at Stanford with us also, was heading back east with his wife, Annette, and they had a great flat in San Francisco. Their landlord lived right above them and was a real asshole. Scott figured that the way to get even with the landlord was to let me have the flat when he left. Scott knew I'd drive that landlord nuts, and that's exactly what we did. Ray and Maryann would come up every weekend, and it was a continuous party. It was amazing the people who would hang out up there. People like S. Clay Wilson, the cartoonist, and some Hawaiian gangsters I had met when I first came to San Francisco. Ray was fascinated by these guys, who would lay their guns out on the table. These were real serious guys.

Aren't we getting close to the time, now, when Ray started to make some attempts to quit drinking?

Well, this is the story I told Tess for the first time just last week when she was here for a visit. It was the first time I felt truly that Ray and Maryann would break up—that it would really happen. Maryann had started to go to AA and she had become involved with someone down there; and back when Maryann had found out about Diane and Ray, she had gone off and had a brief fling with someone else and told Ray about it, and they had gone a couple of rounds over it. So there was a history of violence.

But now they were back together again and over at our place one weekend, before going off for a week of fishing. Maryann was dressed up in a beautiful white dress for dinner. They were talking about the future and waxing nostalgic about the past, but there was a lot of tension going on as the drinking got heavier and heavier. Maryann was trying to keep it afloat, being witty and lively, but I could sense Ray was in a lot of pain. He could become very jealous at times; and when the rage and pain would come from so deep within him it would frighten him to death, and he was leery of it.

Just about then Shorty Ramos, one of the Hawaiian gangsters, showed up and, trying to goad Ray, Maryann started flirting with Shorty. There were a couple of kisses at the table, and things were building up. Then Shorty left and I went to bed, thinking things would cool down. Maryann and Ray were sitting on the couch and my wife, Diane, was sitting across from them. She was just sitting there watching them drink and fight. Diane said you could see the intensity mounting. Then they both stood up, and Maryann said something to Ray, and he hit her on the side of her head with a bottle, and the bottle shattered, glass flying across the room. Maryann ran out of the house and just disappeared. Diane and Ray went out after her. Diane told him to go back in the house and stay there, and he did. Diane then followed a trail of blood and found Maryann standing in an alley, dazed and bleeding profusely. Diane led her back to the house. I woke up when I felt someone squeezing my foot. It was

Maryann, and her white dress was drenched in blood. She said, "Look what Ray did."

I jumped up and got a towel and pressed it to her neck. Diane called for an ambulance, and they took her to the hospital, Diane going with her. Ray and I sat out at the kitchen table, but he couldn't talk. He was devastated by what he had done.

Had you not acted so quickly, Maryann could have died and Ray would have gone to prison. Talk about trusting your accidents. That changed their lives, but it could have been tragic.

No question about it. She would have bled to death. But it was Diane who saved her life. This was as violent as it ever got. There had been black eyes and such, but nothing like this. And after those violent events, there was always such a tenderness between them that was hard to explain. He moved in to stay with us, and Maryann came over after she had been discharged from the hospital. He was sitting there smoking, shamefaced, and you could see the pain in his eyes. Maryann went over to him and placed her hands on the back of his head and gently patted him. She didn't say much. A friend came and picked her up, and she went to stay with her friend.

It's hard to believe they'd ever get back together after this incident; but they did, didn't they?

Yes, a number of times. Funny thing—he couldn't remember hitting her with the bottle. Even years later, after he stopped drinking and we'd get together or talk over the phone, he had no memory of it. On occasion he would ask me questions about that night and all that had happened—who did what and when. I can remember him shaking his old woolly head and saying very Carverish things like, "Who was that person? Who was that person who said he was me? Who was that person using my name?" Those were very strange times. I remember once when we were all out at Ocean Beach and the body of a drowned man washed up not fifty feet from where we had spread our blankets. Really—this actually happened. Diane spotted him first. His eyes were open and fixed. He was a guy of about thirty-five, muscular and handsome, and he had all these tattoos on his arms. Ray and I began bickering on what to do, about who should try to give the poor devil mouth-to-mouth or something, but neither of us moved a muscle. Ray suggested there was a phone in the Beach Chalet bar across the road he could use for help. Sure, Ray. Finally, a man in a red wet-suit tried to give him mouth-to-mouth, for all the good it did. Anyway, later that day Ray and I decided what we needed to do for ourselves was get tattoos. So we sat at the kitchen table for hours drinking and drawing tattoo designs, saying, whatever I drew, Ray would have inked on his skin, and vice versa. I drew something I wanted to look like both a valentine heart and a skull, and I wrote DIANE across it. Then Ray drew a pretty good picture of a real heart—an anatomical heart, not some valentine heart—and he wrote MARYANN in it. Crazy.

Anyway, they kept separating and getting together, and for a while they had a sweet little attic apartment on Castro, that Maryann fixed up as only Maryann can. It was a sweet time for them—maybe the last sweet time. Maryann was going to AA, but Ray was still drinking seriously and in and out of hospitals. He had collapsed in a doctor's office. They gave him several stitches and said he had wet brain. He went up to Duffy's, and Maryann went seriously into AA. And that was when she met a guy there who appears in a couple of Ray's stories.

Is this Ross of "Mr. Coffee and Mr. Fixit"?

Yep, that's him.

Was he an engineer?

Well, he said he was, I guess. First I heard he was an astronaut. Then he was a big rocket engineer. Then it kept getting lower and lower.

Just like Mr. Fixit. Ray says in the story that he had his number when he saw two busted Plymouths in the guy's yard.

Well, Maryann was involved with that guy. She'd go down to see him, and that was upsetting to Ray. They were having an anniversary or something, and Ray had bought champagne and flowers, and then she didn't show up. She comes back two or three hours later, and there's Ray at the top of the stairs with all the flowers torn and ripped up all around him.

That sounds like the kernel for "A Serious Talk."

Could be. They used to go down to Market Street and spend afternoons watching porn movies. They'd have their sweet times together, but it was the last of the sweet times. There were a lot of breakups. Ray went to Duffy's again, and Doug, Amy, and I went to pick him up in Doug's little old red Toyota truck. On the way back, Ray and I rode in the back, bouncing around like a pair of field hands in the bed of that truck, because Doug drove like a maniac. We talked a lot, smoking some dope. Ray smoked dope all his life. He never did quit that. He told me he thought he was real close to having his last drink. And he talked about his father and how his father died—most of which I'd heard before, but not told with such emotion and sadness. When it had happened, his mother called Maryann and told her, out of the blue, that Ray was dead. It took a while for Maryann to realize she was talking about Ray's father, who was also called Ray. Ray talked a whole lot about his father. It was a sad trip back, but by the time we hit the Golden Gate Bridge we were laughing again.

You were talking about the last of their sweet times. Ray wrote a story, "Chef's House," describing their last sweet time together. Could you tell us something about that?

I was coming back with Diane from giving a reading at the writers' conference in Port Townsend, and we stopped to visit them at Chef's house. That was a real sweet time. Neither of them were drinking, but it was a sad time. There was a sense of loss. Another time Diane had received a little money from an inheritance. She wanted to throw a party, of course, so she sent Ray money for round-trip airfare from Iowa City, where he was living then. He bought a one-way ticket, and he used the leftover money to drive Maryann back with him to Iowa.

Didn't he then leave Iowa for El Paso? That must have been their last breakup. What do you know about that?

They had all kinds of problems in Iowa—too much emotional baggage—and that was really the end of their time together. Ray later told me it was Maryann who set him adrift. They had a mournful but loving talk deciding what to do. He had the teaching job lined up in El Paso, and she had some money coming from her teachers' retirement fund. So she was the one who actually said it: "You go off and have a good life in El Paso; I'm going to California." She made the decision. He got into this old car that his son, Vance, had left there and drove off for El Paso. And that pretty much was the end of it. Of course, the car broke down on the way.

Wasn't that where he met Tess again, in El Paso?

Yes, she was a reinforcement in his life—a real steadying influence. She's a strong woman, a class act. Maryann went back to California, and I can't remember the last time I saw her. She cut herself off from all their old friends. Al Young ran into her in a drugstore in Palo Alto many years ago, and she was distant and obviously didn't want to talk. It was her decision to remove herself from our lives, although we still have so much affection for her.

Did you ever hear Ray say that he expected to die young?

Yes, a few times. But it wasn't like a grand, romantic prediction of the artist-dying-young bullshit variety. I think he really believed it. He really did have a premonition, if you believe in those sorts of things. I remember him talking about it one time in particular. I was the writer in residence at the University of Alabama at Tuscaloosa in the spring of 1980, and I arranged for Ray to give a reading. He and Tess were in Syracuse then. At any rate, the day after the reading we took the Southern Crescent train down to New Orleans, where we joined up with Richard and Kristina Ford for a holiday. Richard had a room reserved for Ray and me in a great little hotel on Toulouse, right off Bourbon Street. We'd all sit out on that balcony at night and sip champagne—except Ray, of course, in the hot dark and tell lies. We had a great few days together. One afternoon, Ray and I were knocking around the Quarter when it began to pour rain, so we ducked into this museum off of Jackson Square and started wandering around. We came upon an exhibit of a death mask of Napoleon, and Ray was absolutely fascinated by it. I had to drag him away. Later that night, Ray and I pulled chairs up to the big window that overlooked the courtyards in back, put our feet up, and watched the rain while we passed joints and bullshit back and forth. It was then that he told me for the first time how close he'd come to committing suicide after he quit drinking and thought he'd never be able to write again. He talked about Tessie a lot that night, too—what all she had meant to him staying sober, and how he thought in a lot of ways she had saved his life. He also kept bringing up that death mask of Napoleon, and maybe he should get fitted for one too before long, because of that old feeling that he wouldn't be around long. At that point Ray had about eight more years, I guess.

Did you keep in touch with him all through his illness?

Yes, of course. As a matter of fact, the summer before he became ill I had a sabbatical and met with him in San Francisco. The plan was for me to stay at his and Tess's house while they went to Europe, but the plans changed. They went to Europe and came back and were about to go again when Diane bought this house, so that took care of that plan. We got together again later in the summer after he had just finished "Errand." We went up to Davis, where he read it for the very first time. The next morning we had breakfast with Jack Hicks and some students. He was going to read some of the students' stories and talk with them. We hugged and said goodbye, and that was the last time I saw him. I didn't know that at the time.

How did you hear that he was ill?

He called me up and told me. He told me that he had something dark down there. It was going to be hard business, but it had to be attended to. "I'm optimistic, and I'm sure it's going to be fine. It's not my time yet."

I was frightened. But then again, I couldn't imagine anything like that happening to him. What I thought about was that time in New Orleans and how, when he was talking about cashing it in early, I kept busting his chops. I had told him he'd better not croak without leaving me something. Well, he did leave me something—more than he ever knew.

November 8, 1990
Pittsburgh, Pennsylvania

Ray Carver, Richard Ford,
and Kristina Ford in
Port Angeles, 1987.

RICHARD FORD

The stories seemed very fresh to me, and extremely gripping and dramatic. I thought they attempted to give language to things—to moments in life— which, until you read his story, you never realized existed importantly. You knew they existed, but Ray made them hold a great deal—those moments. As with all great work, his stories made you pay atten- tion to life.

Ford and his wife, Kristina, meet me at the door of their splendidly restored 1830s house on Bourbon Street in New Orleans. They greet me warmly, hospitably. He has just arrived the previous day and is trying to recover from the effects of a six-day drive down from their other home in Montana.

It has taken over a year for Ford to agree to this meeting and, though he does his gracious best to make me comfortable, I have more than my usual measure of preinterview apprehension. He answers questions directly with no hesitation. A trace of southern drawl in his high tenor voice does little to deter him from speaking paragraphs at a time in rapid-fire bursts, with an earnest energy that later sparks off a touch of heat once or twice. When you talk Ray Carver and writing with Richard Ford, you're close to touching a piece of his heart.

Later in the evening, as we watch TV, I hear an astute running commentary from the author of *The Sportswriter,* as Mike Tyson takes out an inept, frightened opponent in the first round. We all turn in early. The next morning, as we discuss the interview, Ford expresses uneasiness—a disapproval with what he perceives, on my part as a latent quest for the sensational in a few of the questions. It's over, forget it, he'll not participate in this project.

A dark moment. Smooth sailing, and then here we run into an iceberg. I do what I can to control the damage, and we spend over an hour patching up the mess. There are a few weak areas that could stand amplification. Ford agrees to taping more questions and answers. After lunch, we watch a bit of pro football. When I leave, I know I've caught but a mere sighting of the exposed surface of Richard Ford. The massive remainder is kept well submerged.

Sam Halpert: When and where did you first meet Ray?

Richard Ford: I first met Ray in November, 1977, in Dallas, Texas. It was the same time that I met Tess, in fact. At the time I was a close friend of Michael Ryan, the poet. Michael was teaching at SMU and had asked me to be a part of the Southern Methodist University Writers' Festival. I had published one book and was barely out of the box.

Was that your first novel?

Yes, *A Piece of My Heart.* So I went, and Ray was there. I hadn't any special anticipation of meeting him. I'd read some stories of his in *Esquire,* and liked them. When I was in school in California in the late sixties, his name was around.

Will You Please Be Quiet, Please? *had come out by then. Had you read it?*

No. In fact I hadn't heard much about the book. At the time I wasn't leading much of what you might call a literary life. I was staying home writing. I wasn't paying much attention to *The New York Times.* The world seemed pretty big to me, as it still does. There were people out there writing, and I was happy to be among them. Ray had read some things of mine, or said he had. I think he may have read part of *A Piece of My Heart* which was published in *Esquire.*

Your book and Ray's book came out about the same time?

Yes, my book was published in '76 and Ray's book came out the same year. But we just hit it off. When we met, there was this sense of— here's a man I like. He was living at the time in Arcata, and had been off of drinking for a while. I can never remember whether Ray went off the booze in June of '76 or '77. I know he hadn't been off it for long. There was an understanding among people around him that he had been a bad drinker, a provisional attitude having to do with how long he'd be able to hold off drinking. Indeed, when I met him, he hadn't had a drink in some good while, and he never did again that I'm aware. But he shared that provisional attitude—about himself. He was taking one day at a time.

So that was the beginning; how did it continue?

Yes, that was the beginning. We hit it off right from the start. I was living in Princeton at the time. And in the ensuing months, we became friends. With other people—including Michael Ryan—I helped Ray get a job at Goddard. What I mean by help, is that I vouched for him. Geoffrey Wolff I'm sure did, too. We vouched on no surety except that we liked Ray and liked his stories, and that Ray would come to Goddard and teach, and would not get drunk and disappear—which, indeed, he didn't do. He came to Goddard and was a wonderful teacher and it all worked out fine. This was in January '78.

That was an all-star group up there that year. There was Carver and you and Toby and Geoffrey Wolff—

And Michael Ryan and John Irving and Craig Nova and Donald Hall and George Chambers and Robert Hass and Ellen Voigt and Louise Gluck. Of course, that putative star-quality is meaningless. I just think of those people as they were: my friends. And most still are.

How did you follow up with Ray after the session at Goddard?

After Goddard, Ray came down to Princeton and stayed with Kristina and me for a week.

Is that when you got that farmhouse for him in Illinois?

No, I didn't get that place for him in Illinois. He got that himself. He got it from Curt Johnson, who published *December* magazine. Anyway, when he left Princeton, he went to this house in Illinois. It seemed like a good idea to him. He wanted to write, and he seemed to have the drinking beaten. But he got out there and very quickly found he didn't want to stay. He hated it out there.

It was February and he was isolated.

He was isolated and felt cold as hell. As soon as he got out there, the weather cracked down on him, and he left. I think of it now as being that provisional time—still. He was a bit on the move, didn't have a lot of money. I think he and Maryann were separated, at least *de facto*. He was looking to be still in a place where he wouldn't get the willies. In retrospect, he was warding off the impulse to take a drink, I guess.

I believe that's when he returned to Iowa City.

That must have been when he stayed with Stephen Dobyns. I'm a third party to all that. But it was beginning to be clear that Ray was pulling himself together. He was working hard and writing stories. We talked on the phone often and he seemed utterly himself—by that I mean the way he always would be after that—cheerful, eager, generous.

Regarding Maryann—did you have much contact with her?

Virtually none. They were separated at the time. At least, I guess they were. I don't think they got divorced until 1982. They had been through a lot of travail together, and he loved her very much; but they just hadn't been able to live with each other any longer. He said that to me many times during this period. However, Ray was the kind of guy that, if there was bad news floating around, he didn't tell it to you. He didn't cry on your shoulder. In fact, he was quite secretive. I remember only once that Maryann called, to say she was having that birthday party for Ray, his fortieth, and could we come. But we couldn't. I can't remember where that party might have taken place.

The invitation was for you and Kristina?

Yes. Kristina and I were like a unit to Ray, and he took us both on. There was a sense of mutuality, which was quite sweet.

Did you see Ray and Maryann together?

Not while Ray was alive. I saw them together when Ray was dead.

That's when I first met you, in Montana. You had just come from Ray's funeral. Could you say anything about that?

Well, having been to a lot of funerals in my life, I didn't find it to be much out of the ordinary. Out of the ordinary maybe only in one sense—that Tess not only allowed but invited Maryann and Chris and some of Maryann's immediate family to the funeral. Tess was just trying to say that this is your ex-husband and this is your father, and we all loved him, and now he's gone, and we have to bury him, and I don't want to exclude you. It was very generous of her. Other than that, no, there wasn't anything unusual.

That's remarkable. Was there much drinking?

At the funeral? I don't remember. But there was food. It was all in the American tradition in which the neighbors bring pies. It's a little like Christmas, except somebody's dead. Other than that, how people express their grief, and the stresses that grief places on people— particularly in familial situations such as Ray's was—all that is private.

Well, everyone there loved him deeply, and were under heavy emotional strain, and it was a great shock—

It wasn't a great surprise. We knew he was dying.

I said shock. I mean although they expected him to die, there was always the hope that perhaps he'd recover, but what they had to deal with now was the reality—

Well, as I said, Ray kept the most grievous things to himself if he could. The last month of his life, perhaps the last two months of his life. he pretty much packed it in. He kept to himself and Tess. The goings and comings of his day-to-day life were pretty much just the two of them together. He worked hard, we now know. I talked to him fairly often during that period—not as often as usual. I remember he called me up one day and told me that his son, Vance, was there. Vance had come in from Germany. Ray sounded quite agitated. His kids agitated him. He loved them, but they agitated him. He said, "Look, I'm going to put Vance on the phone. Would you talk to Vance?" I said, "Sure, I'll talk to Vance." And I talked to Vance about what—I don't even remember. We just talked. I've known Vance since he was a teenager, and I like him very much. I think Ray just wanted Vance to know, in some very indirect way, that he had a friend in me. I only talked to Ray a couple of times after that. It must have been mid-June, 1988.

During this period of time, Ray was telling all the reporters and writers that he had this thing licked, that he was coming out of it. And of course he hadn't. What was he telling you?

Nothing explicit. I think it was a tenet of our friendship that I wouldn't ask him if there weren't some special reason, and there wasn't. I knew he'd had a recurrence in the winter before, in February, and I knew he'd had another recurrence. It was typical of me, and typical of our friendship, that I wasn't keeping tabs on him. I wasn't calling him up and taking his pulse all the time, because I wanted to try, and he wanted to try, to keep normal life going.

It wasn't exactly denial, but nevertheless you didn't want to—

No, I'm not a denier of things like that, and he wasn't in a position to deny anything. The last time I laid eyes on him he looked like hell, I know that. He was very puffy and bloated. There was no denial. He had just so many days left to live and wanted to get the most out of them—not succumb to gloominess.

Where was that?

At the American Booksellers Association in June at Anaheim. We gave a reading together. It was the last reading he ever gave. He was going on with things.

And at that time he was telling people he was recovering.

He seemed troubled to me. I remember saying to him, "Look, Curley"—I used to call him Curley. I said "You seem fine to me, you look fine. This is all going to work out right." And he looked at me and said in a very grave voice, "Well, I hope so," which was the least hopeful words I'd ever heard him say.

140

You were his friend. At the same time, he was telling others that he had this thing licked.

He had not long come back from the doctors at that time, and he'd been told that he was dying, that he wouldn't live very long. This was maybe three weeks before he and Tess got married. I don't know what he was telling the world about his illness. He did not tell me, though, that he'd been given the black spot.

What was your reaction to their marriage?

I tend to be kind of blithe about people's decisions to get married. But there was much more poignance to the situation than was apparent to me at the time. I was in Salt Lake City, and I was supposed to fly over to Reno to be their witness, but I couldn't. The timing was just impossible.

Do you regret not going?

No, it's much better that I didn't go. I would have loved to have done that with them, but, really, that was something that they were happiest to do alone. They would have included me, if it could have worked out, but given the fact that it was so near to his death, it was far better that they did that by themselves. They were very close.

We've jumped quite a ways. Let's see, I think we were talking about the time he went back to Iowa City. Where did you pick up on him after that?

I think the next time was at Goddard for the summer session. I wasn't teaching there then, but I was there to give a reading. Kristina and I had left Princeton and moved to Pownal in Vermont. After Goddard, Ray spent a week with us. From there, he went out to Iowa City again, and that time he was on his way to El Paso where he had a teaching job. And on his way down to El Paso, that was when the old car that Vance had left him finally broke down completely.

Down in Van Horn, Texas. The story he liked to tell was that he traded it for a bicycle

[Laughs.] You can bet that isn't true. Ray pedaling a bicycle, that would be the day! Unless the bicycle was on a track to a dough-nut shop.

Yeah, he probably just junked the car.

Sure, he junked it right there and never saw it again. He took the bus on into El Paso. I was in touch with him a lot, particularly in the first semester in El Paso. I remember very vividly talking him out of quitting his job at mid-year. I remember him saying that he didn't like it there and he didn't want to stay.

Was it because he didn't like teaching, or did he have other reasons?

I don't know. He just didn't like being there. It very well could have been that he had connected with Tess by that time, and wanted to move up to Tempe. What went on between him and Tess between the fall of '77 and the fall of '78, I don't know.

A love affair?

A love affair, yes, but I wasn't privy to it. I just kept saying to him, "Look, don't quit this job. With this job, you can go on and get another better job. So don't quit it, because it will go hard for you if you don't stay in El Paso, and you want to go someplace better." Indeed, by that time, he was trying to get a job at Syracuse. George Elliott, who taught at Syracuse, loved Ray's work but was a little skittish of Ray because of his drinking past. I remember calling and telling George that Ray was a stand-up guy, and "as soon as you meet him, you'll love him." And, indeed, when George did meet him, he took to him immediately, and Ray took to George, and they were great friends until George died.

So Ray went to Syracuse and set up his own little Mafia there.

[Laughs.] Well, I don't know. But, if so, he was a very negligent Don.

[Laughs.] *No, somehow I can't see Ray as a Godfather.*

No, Ray didn't enjoy teaching. He wanted to be writing.

But look at all his pals he brought in.

Yes, Tess and Toby and Doug, Stephen Dobyns. Hayden Carruth came at the same time Ray did.

Wasn't this about the time he'd got back to his writing?

Just before Ray went to Syracuse, he sent me a whole batch of stories in manuscript—about five, I believe. These stories were written in sort of a spate—maybe even six stories. I remember I didn't like a couple of them, or I had some things to say about them which weren't entirely praising.

Would it be fair to ask the names of those stories?

One was called "The Calm." I didn't like it very much.

Was that the one narrated in a small town barber shop?

Yes. Anyway, I wrote him a long letter and told him all about it. Needless to say, there was a preponderance of praise too.

What was the other story?

I don't remember. This was in a bunch that included "Tell the Women We're Leaving." I had some critical things to say, but he'd sent me these stories and I thought he wanted some comment. So I told him some things, and he never showed me another story as long as he lived. *[Laughs.]* Criticism—even of a friendly variety—was not what he wanted to hear at all.

Do you remember your criticism of "The Calm"?

Yeah. I was specific about "The Calm" because it was a story that had an envelope to its structure. The first-person narrator tells about another person's story.

A frame?

Yes, I didn't think the story had a closing frame on the backside. The story doesn't end outside the interior story, and I thought he should try that. Some sense of symmetry caused me to comment on it. I still feel the same way about it. For a while I needled Ray good-naturedly about that. Eventually he sent me the book, and I said that I liked it all but "The Calm." He'd always laugh and say I was wrong and that he'd received more praising letters about that story than any story he ever wrote. It became a joke between us. At first it wasn't a joke, but then it became a joke. He knew I loved his work. The story was published in the *Iowa Review.*

Ethan Canin told me that when he was editing the Iowa Review, *they printed a story of Ray's, leaving off the last line by error.*

What did they do about it?

I think they printed the last line in the next issue.

[Laughs.] I'll bet that didn't bother Ray a bit!

When you say you loved his work, what is there in the work that you love?

The stories seemed very fresh to me, and extremely gripping and dramatic. I thought they attempted to give language to things—to moments in life—which, until you read his story, you never realized existed importantly. You knew they existed, but Ray made them hold a great deal—those moments. As with all great work, his stories made you pay close attention to life.

Was that what made it a Carver story?

I suppose. He would tell you something, and then he'd tell you something else, and then he'd tell you something else. And every time he'd go to the next, to the next, to the next. It was surprising, dramatic, extremely informative emotionally. As soon as you realized what he'd told you, you realized the great hazardous possibility of overlooking those things—in ordinary life moments, small events, utterances—and that for our humanity to survive they needed to be observed. The other thing I loved about his work is that I thought it was very funny. *Very* funny. I've seen him give readings of the story "What We Talk About When We Talk About Love," and there's a moment there when the character makes a noise like a bee, "b-zzzz b-zzzz." I've heard Ray read that story aloud and start laughing. Again, he managed to do what great writing does, to deliver the fullest array of human response to complicated life. In that way it was often very instructive work.

When you say he inspired laughter in his readings—

He made himself laugh, as well as his listeners.

I once attended a reading of "Intimacy"—

You know, I said to him after I read that story, "Jesus, Ray," I said, "I read your story about Maryann." That's very unlike me. It's unlike me because I recognize and I insist in my own work that direct correlations between life and what gets represented in stories are impossible, untrue. And I didn't even know Maryann, but this remark just leapt out of my mouth. I said, "I read the story about Maryann." And he said in a very guarded way, "That wasn't about Maryann." And then I thought to myself after I said that, "Well, that's right. Even if it's not right, it's right."

Could you clear that up for me?

Well, I really knew practically nothing—certainly nothing more than what he told me—about their life, his and Maryann's, or about the time they spent together after they were divorced. I don't know anything at all about that. I had no reason to think it was about Maryann, except that the story was so authentic sounding.

Didn't it ring true to everything you'd heard about him and Maryann?

It rang true to everything I knew about Ray. *[Laughs.]*

Do you think Ray wrote that story with humorous intent?

I don't know. I would say that, if that story originated in anything like what it represents to be, that when the original events were taking place there was no humor in it. When he wrote it, though—Ray was a very astute craftsman of his stories and authored every effect, so I can't believe that he didn't know there were many funny things in this story.

You know Ray seemed in many ways like a *natural*. And to a certain extent, he was kind of a natural. But he was also scrupulous and thoughtful and careful and knew literature from the heart, from the gut, as well as from the mind. What he loved he loved intensely and studied intensely, so I believe he could only know every ramifying effect of his stories.

What you've just said makes me think of the line in "Intimacy" where, after being raked over the coals by his ex-wife, the narrator says, "Make no mistake, I feel I'm home."

I think that's one of the balming effects of his work. His stories always seem to talk about grave things, but there's always something that you can take away with a sense of benefit. Not a message, but just something you can use.

There's one story of his that always bothers me: "Popular Mechanics." What's that story all about?

What's the last line? "In this manner the issue was decided." As to what that's all about, there's only one person who could've answered that.

Ray's last story, "Errand"—I thought I could always recognize a Ray Carver story

You can't, though—by which I don't mean that you can't sometimes recognize a story of his by its "style." But you couldn't *always* do it. He could surprise you. His work—his style—changed. That's an unfortunate thing about the terms *Carver country* or *Carveresque* as a putative literary description. Most of the sightings that people took on Ray's style—by which I mean, particularly, the length and cadence of his sentences, the length of his stories—those sightings mostly are from *Will You Please Be Quiet, Please?*—his first book.

Do you believe they are overlooking his later work?

Well, *What We Talk About When We Talk About Love,* his next book, contained stories of longer duration, sentences of less clipped cadences. Some stories in that book were edited and revised so that they *seemed* superficially more like earlier stories. But I'd already seen them in manuscript, and I knew them in the original. Gordon Lish *may* have had a hand in those changes, but they were finally Ray's responsibility. But by the time Ray's third book of stories *[Cathedral]* had been published, not only was Gordon out of the picture as editor, but the kind of normal changes that go on in any writer's style as one gets older and learns more and uses things up, and as the demands on one's sentences become different and perhaps greater—these changes were evident. The style and cadence of Ray's sentences had changed. He could still write *short* short stories, but he could do more, too— and would've done a great deal more.

People who love Ray's stories sometimes remember them as seeming more alike than they really are; as in all things, love often prospers through the agency of a kind of restrictiveness. But Ray was a more various writer than many of his fans give him credit for. His sympathies enlarged. As he became, in his life, more comfortable and had a more ample life, his stories became more ample.

As you say, the stories did become longer, more complex, and take on deeper meaning. However, at the risk of oversimplification, they were still about these guys trying to deal with the stuff of their lives—their money problems, their drinking, their women. Then in his last story, ["Errand"] we are suddenly no longer in Carver country. We are strangely somewhere else. What's your sense of that change?

It would have seemed perfectly normal had Ray lived and written another collection of stories. Change, particularly to change by virtue of broadening one's reach, is something all writers know they must do and should do. But you can't just do it by personal fiat. You have to be at the right place at the right time; you have to be submissive to the change; you must have a changing subject matter which you can make your own. Like all good things for writers, much is fortuitous. And I think that in Ray's writing that story *["Errand,"]* lightning struck. It was a sign of things to come—not that he was going to write a series of stories on literary subjects; but he was feeling in that story a kind of exhilaration, a freedom which would've resulted in wonderful work.

Exhilaration?

Ray had a passion and reverence for literature, and particularly for Chekhov. I think he grafted himself onto that piece of Chekhov biography in the same way he had grafted himself onto the bits of life that he knew personally. He just made that be his own.

That story wasn't just Chekhov.

No, but it wouldn't be a story if it weren't Chekhov. If the guy dying in bed of TB were someone else, it would be something different. I can't even remember the title most of the time. I always think of it as the Chekhov story.

Or the story of the waiter.

Ray's stories are often about third parties—people looking out windows, glimpsing what seems to be real life in progress.

In this case, while the rest of the world and the reader is concerned with Chekhov dying in his bed, Ray's eye is on the poor waiter staring at the champagne cork on the floor.

Everyone I've contacted in preparing this book spoke fondly, even lovingly of Ray. What was the quality that made him so likable?

When Ray was around there was such a sense of mirth and good humor in the air—something I don't think I'll ever replace. He was a man able to know the worst about you and find good in you irrespective. The parts that were indelibly good (if you had any) he would absorb and respond to. If he liked you, he liked you. If you got off track, he'd find a way to bring you back to his affection. He was a good man to tell your stories to.

How was he on jokes?

It was an odd thing about Ray. He didn't particularly like jokes, and I do like jokes. I told Ray a lot of jokes until I just figured out that he wouldn't respond. It was as though the factitiousness of jokes couldn't compete with the factual humor of life. Even though Ray was an artist and cared very much about making things, his toehold was in real life. Certainly in a lot of Ray's stories—not in all of them, but many—there was a very pronounced sense—it's part of their illusion—that this is about as close as language can come to representing actuality.

Is that what prompted you to say to him that you had read his story about Maryann?

That remark simply indicated how actual the story seemed. I didn't entirely mean to suggest that I thought that was the case, but that the story seemed so actual.

Well, somehow it was.

What do you mean it was?

I mean that the sentiments that he expressed in the story were feasibly close to those he had in his mind about his relationship with Maryann.

Maybe; maybe not. Anyway it doesn't matter much.

Well, stories just don't come out of thin air.

But in a way they do come out of thin air. If you read a story of mine, or anybody else's, and you ask if I ever knew anybody like this, the answer may be absolutely no. Or did you ever hear anybody say this line? The answer may be "Absolutely no, I made it up." Fiction is made up.

Certainly. But why is your fiction your fiction, and Ray's fiction his fiction, and Lenny Michaels' fiction his? Every writer has his story to tell that comes from out of his experience.

There's a line from Henry James that says, "Experience is sensibility." That's a remark which hopes to blur the relation between fiction and precedent event.

And sensibility comes from what you have lived through. Look, I'm sorry, I don't want this to appear like an argument. I'll cut it out.

No, leave it in. Stories are basically made up of language, not of events. They aren't made of things you've done. They may sometimes seem to refer to things you've done.

Or seen.

Or seen—but committed to language. They can just as often, though, be language that represents absolutely nothing you've ever done or seen or thought about.

I believe that, Richard. I also believe you write the way you do because of everything that has happened to you in your life.

But that's a truism.

Well then, it's true. I'm glad you didn't say that it was sheer bullshit.

[Laughs.] It's not bullshit. It's bullshit's sneaky cousin, a truism.

[Laughs.] *Ray's stories were based on his experience—*

[Emphatically] I don't concede that. I don't concede that because you weren't there, and neither was I.

No, I wasn't. But these interviews demonstrate that you have your perspective on Ray, and Toby Wolff has his, which is similar but still different than Geoffrey's, and Tess Gallagher has hers, and Bill Kittredge has still another. Everyone I interviewed sees Ray through his own periscope. But what seems to emerge from all this is that Ray was able to—and here I don't believe I'm diminishing his art—

You may be, actually, by shifting attention away from it.

No, I don't believe I am. Again, I'm going to have to cut some of this out.

No, leave it in.

What I'm trying to say is that all one has to do is try to do what Ray did, and they'll soon discover how impossible it is. Ray's power was in the way he could examine his experience and create art based on it.

That just isn't a formula that I have any respect for.

I don't see it as a formula.

Well, it's formulaic: You have a life. You make art out of life. That leaves out too much, too much that goes into making stories.

But when you say make art out of life—God! To make art out of anything is such a difficult task. To make art out of life—there's the challenge, it seems to me. I'm not talking about case histories.

I just don't like the notion of Ray making art out of life because, in that way of expressing it, he's responsible to life more than he's responsible to art. I've always supposed that Ray, as a writer, was responsible principally to the integrity of his stories—this even though he *may* have believed the most memorable, ringing things that lived in his life were not stories but lived life. At any point in writing of "Intimacy," I believe his fidelity is to the best next line he can write. That line may have some vagrant origin in experience transmuted by memory and the demands of writing sentences, but it may be absolutely out of no experience. It may be something whose origin he has no idea of, except it comes in his mind—like a little lightning bug. And as long as that's true—and I know that it *is* true— I would say stories are best thought of as being made up and not wedded to life except, of course, after they're made and the reader takes them back to his or her life.

I recognize that. What I mean is—the word that comes to mind is the word impulse. *For instance, the impulse to write "Intimacy." Of course he didn't have to actually visit Maryann to write that story. He visited her in his mind. He's at his keyboard, alone in his room, writing a story. And he's saying, I am visiting her—I say to her such and such. The whole story is a monologue of a narrator's remembered conversation with his ex-wife.*

I simply disagree with all of that.

I trust you don't believe I am denigrating Ray's achievement.

No, but I prefer sticking up for the primacy of imagination, rather than the importance of prior experience. Okay, sure, Ruskin wrote, "You cannot have a landscape by Turner without having a country for him to paint." But I'm just interested in the painting. And as for writers, all I know is that we write one line, then another line, then another.

I don't believe I diminish a writer's creativity when I admire his gift to make art out of his life experience. Look, if all there was to writing a story was in the telling, you could go down to the corner filling station, and sooner or later someone will tell a story that will knock your socks off. Writing the story, though, is an entirely different matter. Ray was able to write stories that evoked in us the same emotional response, as though the story had been told directly to us by someone we cared about.

Maybe. I would certainly have to have him tell me the story in order to answer that. I try to isolate my responses to a story to the facts of them. I like them better that way.

Then I must go back to ask if he created his stories out of thin air.

By which you mean if he writes about a bankrupt, was he ever a bankrupt? My guess is that a lot of things Ray did in one way or another provoked the stories. But beyond saying that, I don't know any more. Only he knew, and I don't care; because to me all that matters is that I read the story. I don't care if Ray had those specific experiences. I just happen to know that once you've committed something to language—experience of any kind—language alters it. There was a trick that Robert Lowell used to play (it's in the Hamilton biography) when trying to perfect a line in a poem, and he couldn't get it right. One of the things he did was put the word "not" in front of the verb, which reversed the meaning of the sentence. But it also added a beat to the line. I think Ray cared more about adding a beat to the line than representing actually, or adequately, or even tangentially or remotely, what actually happened. Ray was an artist when he sat down to write. If it meant tampering with actuality, lying about it, perverting or distorting it, saying x was y and y was x, he'd do it to make a better story. Consequently, to my mind, tracing things back to life is idle. It's to me, gossip of a not very informative kind—even of a misleading kind.

[Short break.]

Some critics say Ray kept writing the story of his life—

That's one more arrogant disservice to his work. There are many others more pernicious than that. I don't find much interest in psychologizing writers. I don't like to be psychologized myself.

I don't suppose it's some critics' function to be mindful.

No. Just to be fair and smart. *[Laughs.]*

Then what does the word minimalism *in regard to Ray's work summon up for you?*

Nothing at all.

Geoffrey Wolff's answer to that question was, "Bullshit."

He *would* say it better than I do. *[Laughs.]*

All the others I interviewed had their own little tale to tell about Ray. They're often funny but somehow always show that endearing quality of his that all remember and miss so much.

Well, I remember at SMU. the day after I had met Ray, I knew I'd met a guy I liked. On the morning after I had met him, I was in my hotel room, asleep actually, and the phone rang. Ray was on the phone. It was the first call I ever got from Ray, and he seemed jittery. He said, "Richard, would you mind coming over to my room?" I asked why. He said, "There's a woman downstairs in the lobby, and she's coming up to my room and I don't want to be alone here with her." I thought that was very funny and agreed to come over. And so here were two guys sitting on the bed, shooting the breeze, when this woman came up. I didn't know who she was. I was the sort of duenno for that little meeting. After an uncomfortable period of time, much to Ray's relief, the woman left. I guess that was a nice entree to Ray's life, though I never knew what had gone on with the two of them. He was a kind of rascal in a way. He was always trying to cope in the present with his occasionally rash acts in the past. That's natural in all human beings, but it was particularly vivid with Ray.

That story seems so characteristic of Ray. Bill Kittredge tells how, shortly after meeting him, Ray was up in Montana for a visit; Chuck Kinder tells of Ray knocking on his door the day after meeting him; and you getting this phone call the day after meeting him. Everyone speaks of his genuine shyness, but I suppose once he considered you as his friend he could drop his guard.

Ray had no difficulty making friends, and he valued friends a lot; though if you ever betrayed him, as a few people did in his life, he held it against you fiercely and forever. I think back in the days when he met Bill and Chuck, he was drinking, and he was on the run from a difficult domestic situation; so it's not surprising that he'd seek solace with his friends—especially when you consider they were writers he admired, and about the same age. One of the things that drew Ray to people was a sense of mutuality: unspeakable things you have done and wanted to be forgiven for; recognizing opportunities you'd seized to be generous; or wanting to do one thing excellently. Once you could hook up with Ray along those lines, then you had a connection with him that was very solid. As Ray got older, his life became so full—people wanting to do things for him, wanting him to do things in the world—he became less and less likely to show up at your door.

Jay McInerney remarked to me that Ray, in his modesty, never appreciated the effect he had on younger writers. When Jay was an editor on the Random Review, *he read hundreds of manuscripts, and he perceived nearly all of them as being versions and derivative of Carver stories. Did you see that effect?*

Myself, I don't think it's true that nearly all writers younger than Ray were influenced by him; and I can say that with perfect ease, because my work was affected by him—and, I think, healthily so, I'm glad to say. But Ray never spoke to me in those terms. That may have been due to his modesty—which was genuine—but it also had to do with something Ray knew and cherished. It was that short stories are received forms. Ray didn't write the first one, and neither did Hemingway, nor did Sherwood Anderson or Chekhov. Insofar as it is a form that Ray and I and Jay inherit, it's natural and inevitable that certain influences occur. There's a mentality, particularly among book reviewers in America, which, when it finds evidence of influence in the work of a writer, wants to create a ranking which purports that the work which demonstrates influence is less worthy than the prior work—some spurious sense of purity. I don't think Ray believed that. He believed that influence was natural, that you learn to write stories from other people, from their work. One of the reasons he seemed unaware of his influence was that it was so native to him.

Native to him?

The fact that influence existed, that he was influenced, and that he might influence other writers. He knew he was influenced by John Gardner and writers he admired, John Cheever and Hemingway and Chekhov. He didn't think it was a big deal. He knew many people read his stories, and that would willy-nilly create an influence. All that mattered was that the influence have a good effect, that it might somehow influence some writer to write a good story better. Assessing influence is a lame way to appraise art—although it's easy. I prefer to try to appraise art in absolute terms, and Ray's work was absolutely excellent.

We haven't spoken about his poetry. Some have said that he'd rather write poems than stories.

The last couple of years of his life, he was intent on writing poems. This is just my opinion, but I think it was easier for him to write poems.

Easier to express himself in poetry? Or the actual process?

I think he found poetry more pleasurable because it was less vexatious. I mean, Ray was not a man who enjoyed hard work. *[Laughs.]*

Few of us do.

[Still laughing] Few of us do—right. I remember when Ray came up to visit and Kristina and I were living in Vermont—this was in 1978. We were living in a big refurbished barn owned by a descendant of James McNeill Whistler, and it was quite nice. Ray allowed how nice it was to live out in the woods with wonderful views and wood fires every night, coziness and the whole nine yards. One morning I hooked the trailer to the tractor and, needing a little help, I asked Ray

to come with me. He said "Okay, Okay." He got on the trailer and after we started down the road, he said to me, "Wait a minute. Where are we going?" I said we were going off to cut wood. He said, "Do what?" I repeated, "Cut wood." And he said "Maybe I'd better go back to the house." *[Laughs.]* He didn't like to do any kind of work. I think there were a few occasions when he wished that he did, but his heart was never in it. He'd never walk when he could ride.

What more can you tell me about his interest in poetry?

It's clear to me that Ray loved poetry. He and Tess and I would fetch up together, particularly after they'd established their lives in Port Angeles. We'd sit around at night in Tess' house and read poems aloud to each other. Ray read to me the first time I ever heard it, Richard Hugo's poem, "Degrees of Gray in Phillipsburg." Poetry was very fundamental to what his understanding of literary art was. But I have to think it was something he could do with ease—which isn't to say he cared about it less. He did it because it was easier for him than cranking up the machinery for a short story. Ray could sit around the house of a morning, smoke cigarettes, look out the window, and write a couple of poems that pleased him.

He said that at times he had written ten or twelve poems in a month.

Oh, he did. But when he wrote short stories, he'd start by getting the whole thing out in one bout of writing. He'd try to stay at that story, unstopping until he finished it, starting early in the morning until late at night, trying to get the whole thing out in one continuous utterance.

That could be wearing.

He could do that for a while, but then he needed relief. Ray certainly could have written novels if he'd ever wanted to. There was nothing in him that stopped him from writing novels. I know he was committed to writing a novel when he died, but it wouldn't have surprised me if the very laborious nature of writing a novel wouldn't finally have discouraged him a bit.

Didn't he say in interviews that he was working on a novel?

He may well have been.

Perhaps something may turn up some day.

I certainly have every confidence he could have written a wonderful novel, but I don't think he wanted to that much.

Do you believe that bothered him at all?

Not a bit. You know, there's another spurious dictum of literary life which says that if you write short stories that's fine, but you're not really a writer until you write novels. That's ridiculous. Ray was a wonderful writer writing his stories and poems. He didn't need to write a novel to prove anything. If he wanted to, he would have written it wonderfully.

I mentioned Ethan Canin earlier. He told me he was working on a novel because everyone is after him to write one. It is expected of him.

That's probably the economics of publishing. Novels are supposedly easier to sell to readers than short stories. That may be a prophecy that publishers fulfill themselves.

A Raymond Carver novel would have built-in big sales.

Sure. Cheever wrote *The Wapshot Scandal* and *Bullet Park* supposedly because of publishing pressures.

You are a switch hitter, known for your novels as well as your collection of short stories. They're both hard work. Do you favor one over the other?

No. I don't like qualitative differences over literary forms. If I could write a beautiful sestina, believe me, I would.

I'm glad you said that. Some poets might take umbrage with your earlier statement about short stories being more difficult to write than poetry.

Poets are frequently in the business of taking umbrage. *[Laughs.]* I didn't say poetry was easier. I said it came easier for Ray. It certainly doesn't come easy for me.

I've never seen a poem of yours.

Well, you may not live that long, Sam. *[Laughs.]*

Getting back to safer ground, would you tell me what you think about the titles of Ray's stories?

I always liked his titles, particularly "Will You Please Be Quiet, Please?" They often seemed arbitrary and hooked on to the story; but as titles they seem to be quirky, and affecting, and new. Sometimes, it's true, somebody will mention the title of a story, and I won't know which the hell story it is. I was never a student of Ray's work, though. I've read all the stories maybe only twice in my life. Ray wasn't a great literary figure to me—he was my pal.

Did your pal ever give you a clue as to how he went about choosing those great titles?

I never knew if he was the guy who always dreamed up the titles. I know in the early stories Gordon Lish had a big influence on Ray— in large measure a good influence—and maybe Gordon helped him with a title. But no matter where the title comes from—if you read it on the side of a bus, or your wife suggests it to you—if you stick it on your story, it's your title. I'll never know why he changed the title of one of my most favorite stories, "What Is It?" to "Are These Actual Miles?"

Why didn't you like that title?

Because it gives away the story's best line. Ray was a guy who, although he was very reluctant to take any literary suggestions from me, would listen if he thought the person had his best interest at heart, was very smart, and had good literary judgment. Maybe I fell outside of the box on all of those.

Who were these people he'd listen to?

He would listen to his editors: Chip McGrath at *The New Yorker* for one, a man he admired very much. He certainly listened to Tess. Finally, though, it doesn't make much difference how the stories came into being what they were, because they were his and only his.

What was his general reaction to editors' suggestions?

I really don't know. I think finally he felt he could bounce things off of Tess, and Tess was smart about stories. He felt he had as much help as he needed. It should be said that he published stories in magazines, and they got edited there.

What was your reaction to the first news of his illness?

Earlier in the summer of '87, Kristina and I and Tess and Ray had been to England and France together. We had a very good time, but I noticed Ray looked thin and kind of gaunt. He seemed from time to time to be not completely well. I had a sense that something was amiss with him. Ray was never a healthy-seeming man. He ate horrible things, smoked a million cigarettes, he'd been through the ravages of liquor. He'd given his body a lot of big whacks. Sometimes I'd go over to his house and he'd go to the store and come back with a sack of doughnuts and Twinkies and God knows what else. I'd laugh and say, "Ray, I hated to see you bring that stuff in here," and he'd say, "You'll feel different about it at twelve o'clock tonight." And he was right.

He seemed to have a thing about doughnuts.

Sweets, cakes, that kind of stuff. But, anyway, we used to talk on the phone a couple times a week, and some time in August of '87, over a series of phone calls in which I'd talk to Tess and then to Ray, it was divulged that he'd had a bad chest x-ray and he'd probably need surgery. It was all done in a hush-hush manner, because he was distressed by it, and Ray hated bad news. He'd had enough in his lifetime. All through September he had all kinds of tests, and it was never ascertained that he had lung cancer until he had the surgery.

Could you tell us something about his attitude then?

I remember I was in Boston on a book tour the weekend before he was going in for exploratory lung surgery. I flew over to Syracuse to spend Sunday with him, because he was antsy as hell about the operation and nervous and afraid. Naturally, Toby was there, and of course Tess. I never will forget that when he took me out to the airport when I left, we talked at great length about how he was going to get through it. And once he penetrated the necessary nervousness, he seemed resolved. Ray was a real grownup. That line in his story where he says, "I've seen some things"—well, he'd seen some things, all right, and he knew he was going to see some more. It didn't surprise him. He just hated it—hated it in a way that you can hate bad news and then finally surrender to it and muscle up—which is what he did.

His fears were tragically well founded. Did he ever tell you that he did not expect to have a long life?

Oh, yes. Part of his view of the world was—get it now, seize it now, because we're not going to be around a long time. He didn't mean it in a morbid way, just in a realistic way. He often said he'd died once and came back to life—referring to his drinking—and he felt that the second life was not going to be a long one. I never thought he'd live long. He didn't conduct himself like a man who was planning on a long life—just a good one.

In his beautiful essay, "Friendship," Ray wrote about how he treasured the bond of friendship he shared with you and Toby Wolff. However, he goes on to say in the essay that it doesn't follow that he would give up his place in the lifeboat for you. He may not have expected a long life, but in this essay, at least, it doesn't seem that he was eager to go. The only alternative to burying your friends, he said, was to have them bury you.

Yes, I think he would rather have buried me than have me bury him. He wanted to live.

Others have described the ingenuous pleasure he took in his boat, his house, his Mercedes, after the deprivations of his so-called previous life. What is your recollection of this?

Oh, he wouldn't hesitate to call you up to tell you about his latest good fortune. But he always made it clear that he wanted to share it with you. It was never bragging. The way I and most of his friends felt was that it was ratifying. It meant that a man as earnest and unguileful and as hard-working and accessible as Ray, could make something which the world deemed excellent. It made me feel that it was worthwhile to keep on with what I was doing. I'm sure his other friends felt the same way.

I like your word, ratifying.

Ray was never a writer standing off from me. He was very close to me, so I can't stand back from him. Nor do I want to. My memories of him are very personal. One of the reasons I suppose I haven't written anything about him is that I don't want my memories of him to become fixed, unreflecting. I want them to stay fluid and supple—full as they always were.

December 8, 1990
New Orleans, Louisiana